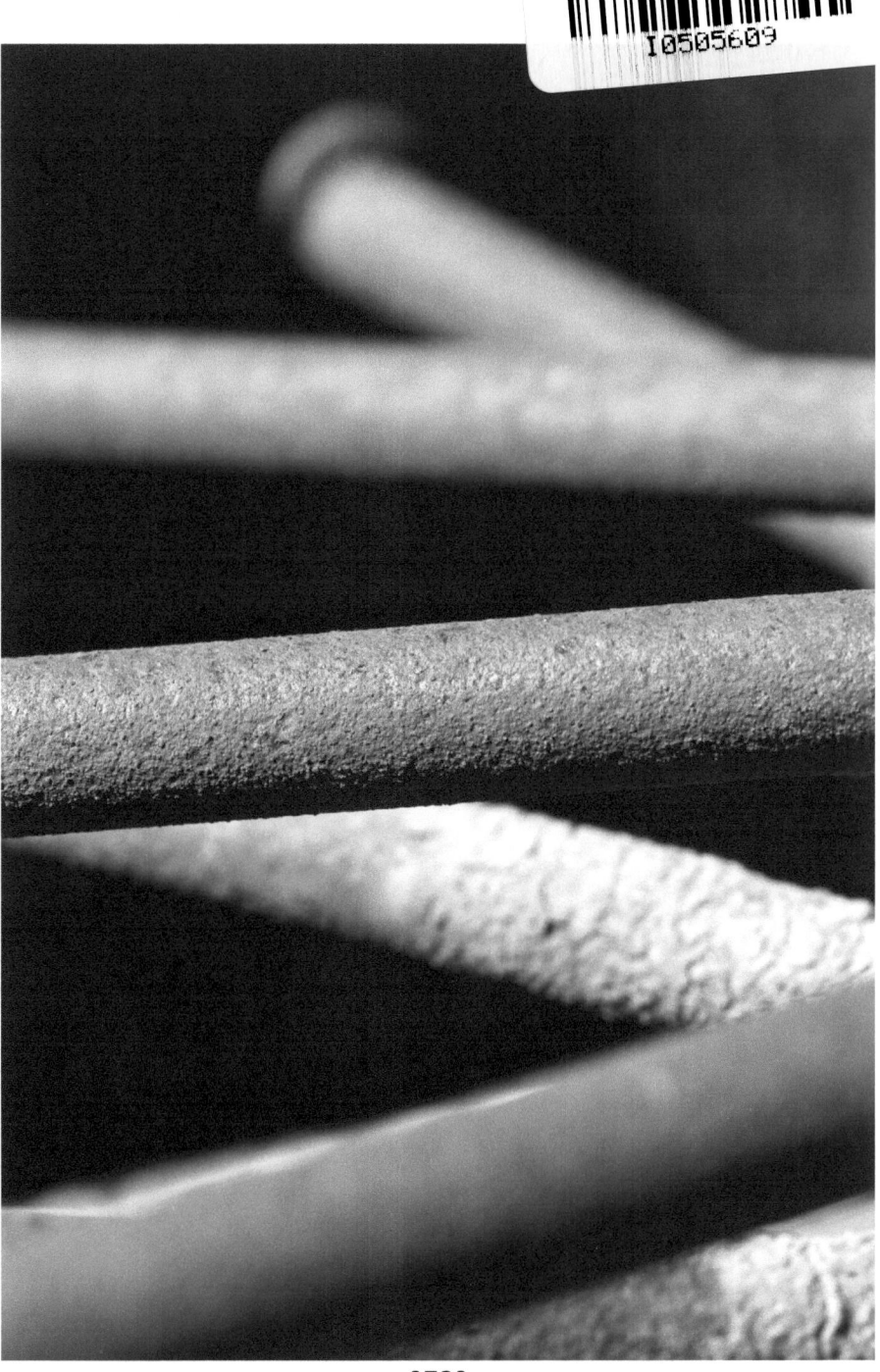

0780

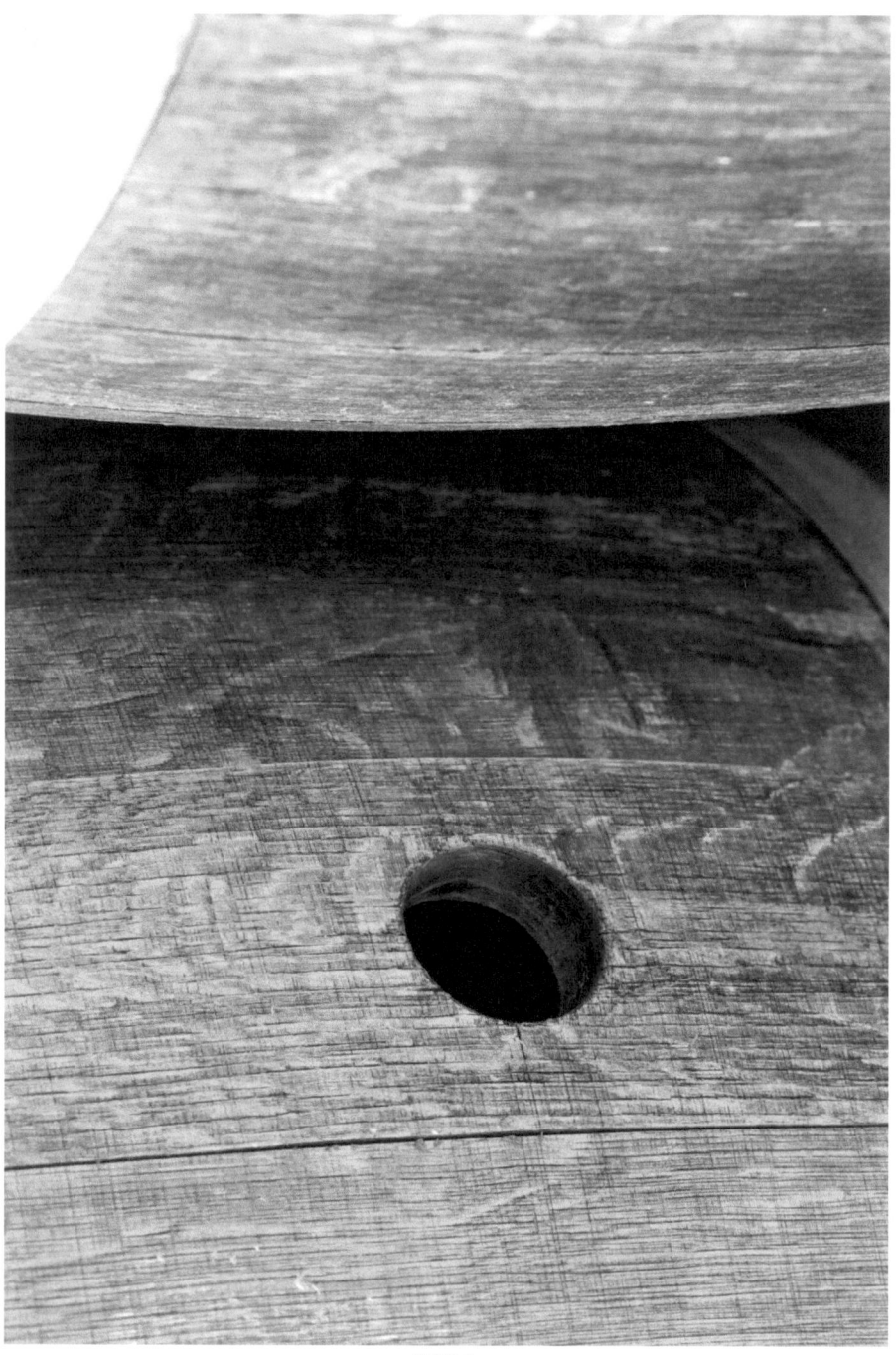

0826

Collected Selections

Decades of being around accomplished talent producing absolutely phenomenal quality work has taught that we are capable of greatness. It is possible to meet our destiny and become it. Experiencing excellence done with such apparent ease and humble selfless gratification is the motivation for this original photography. Most important was having the freedom.

Being colorblind gives an advantage when composing black & white… less confusion. This special collection selected from thousands of captures. All images were framed in the camera and presented without edits, genuine as seen through the lens. RAW conversion applied by proprietary panchromatic process from source files.

Limited edition prints and custom artwork available.

info@ BEACHNOISE.com

Joseph Fleming

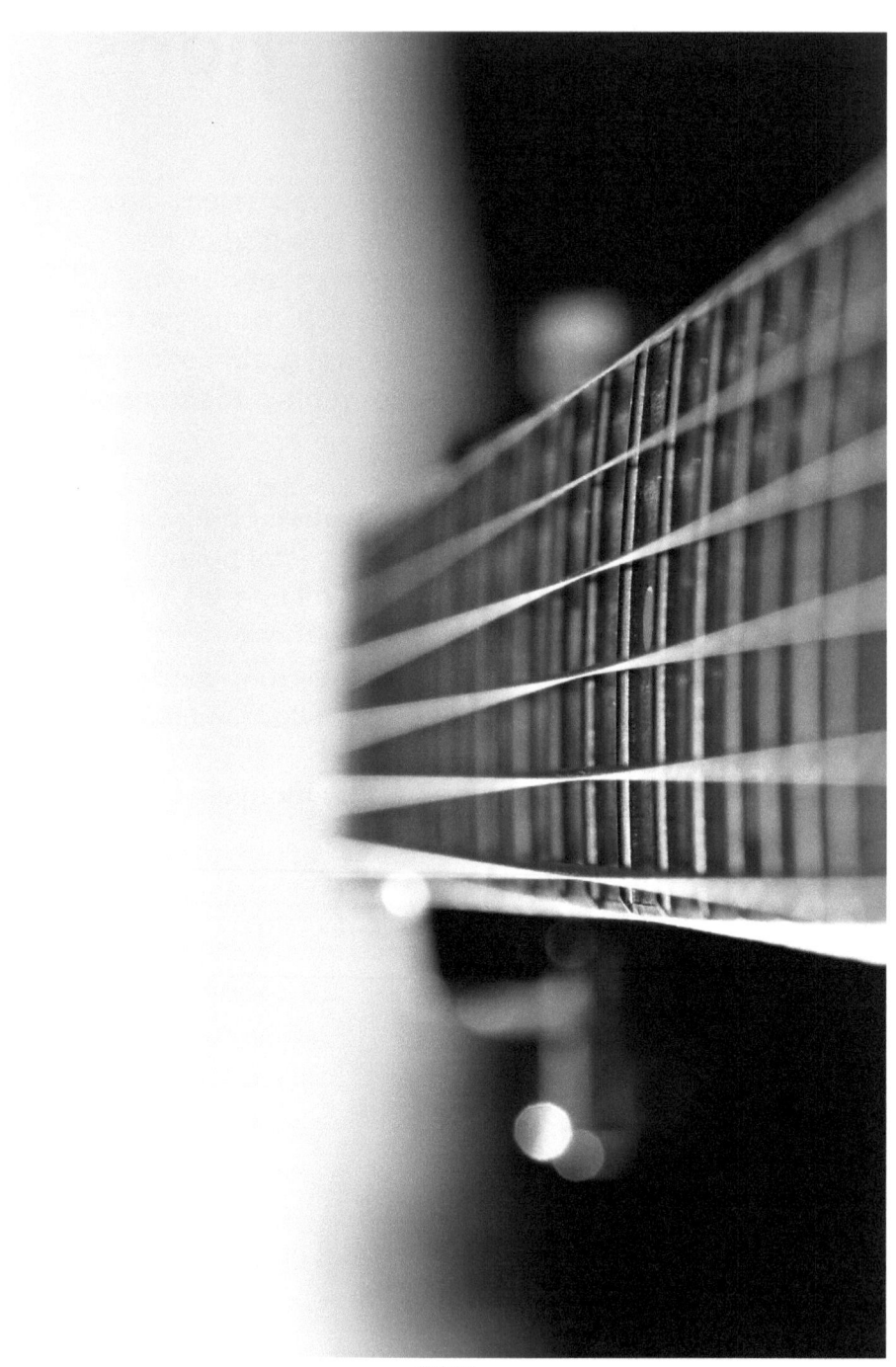

0351

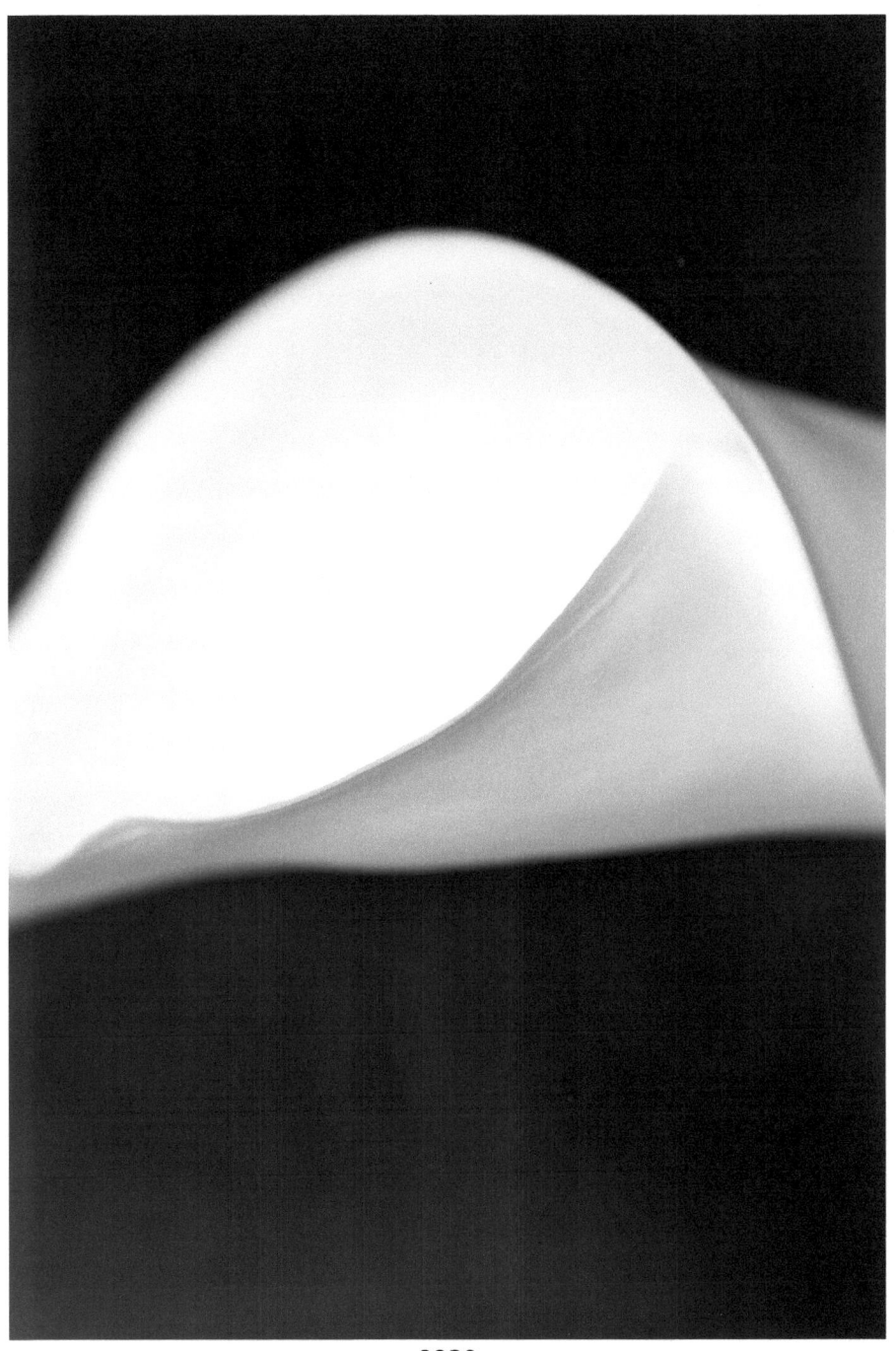

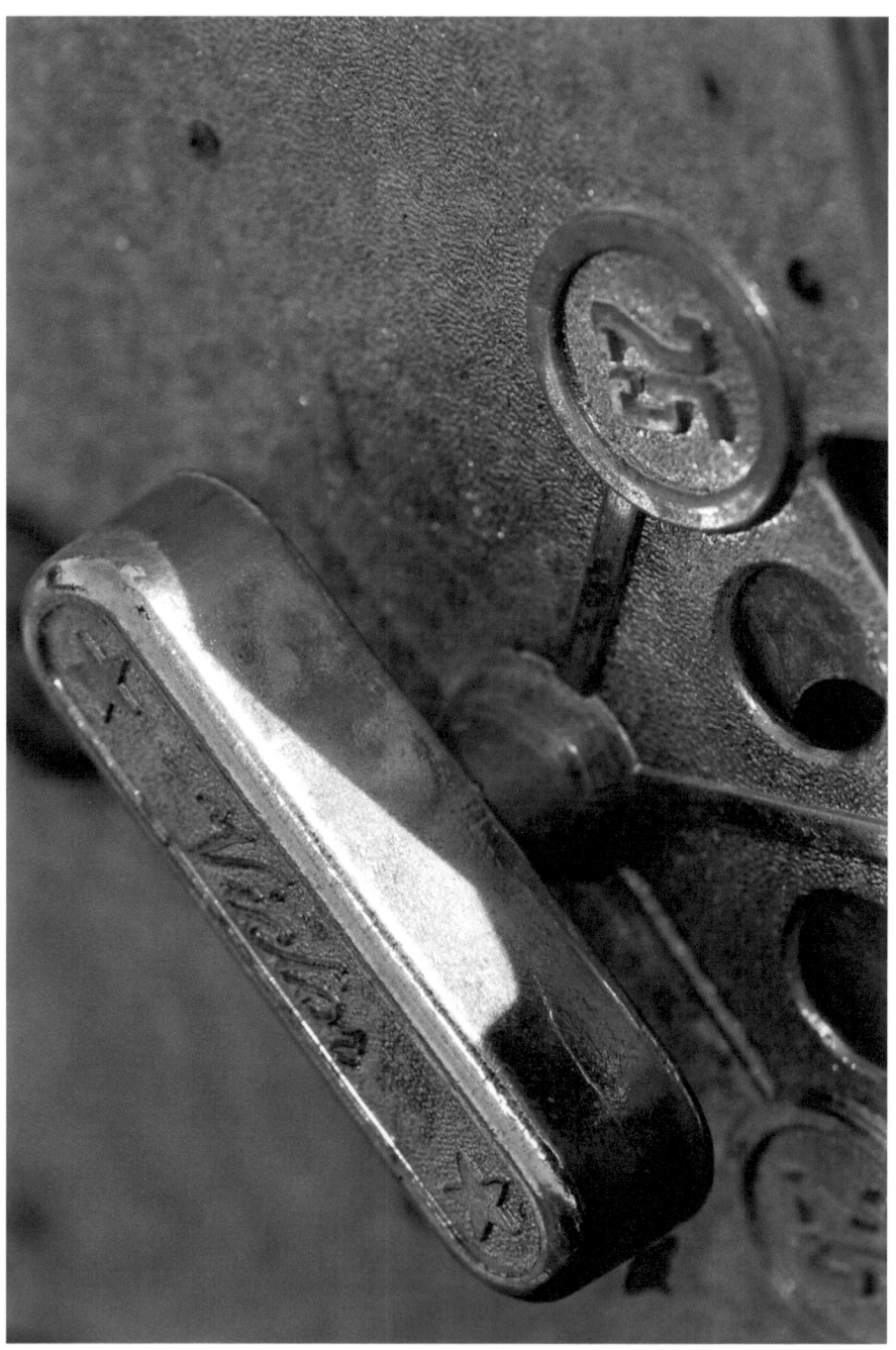

1085

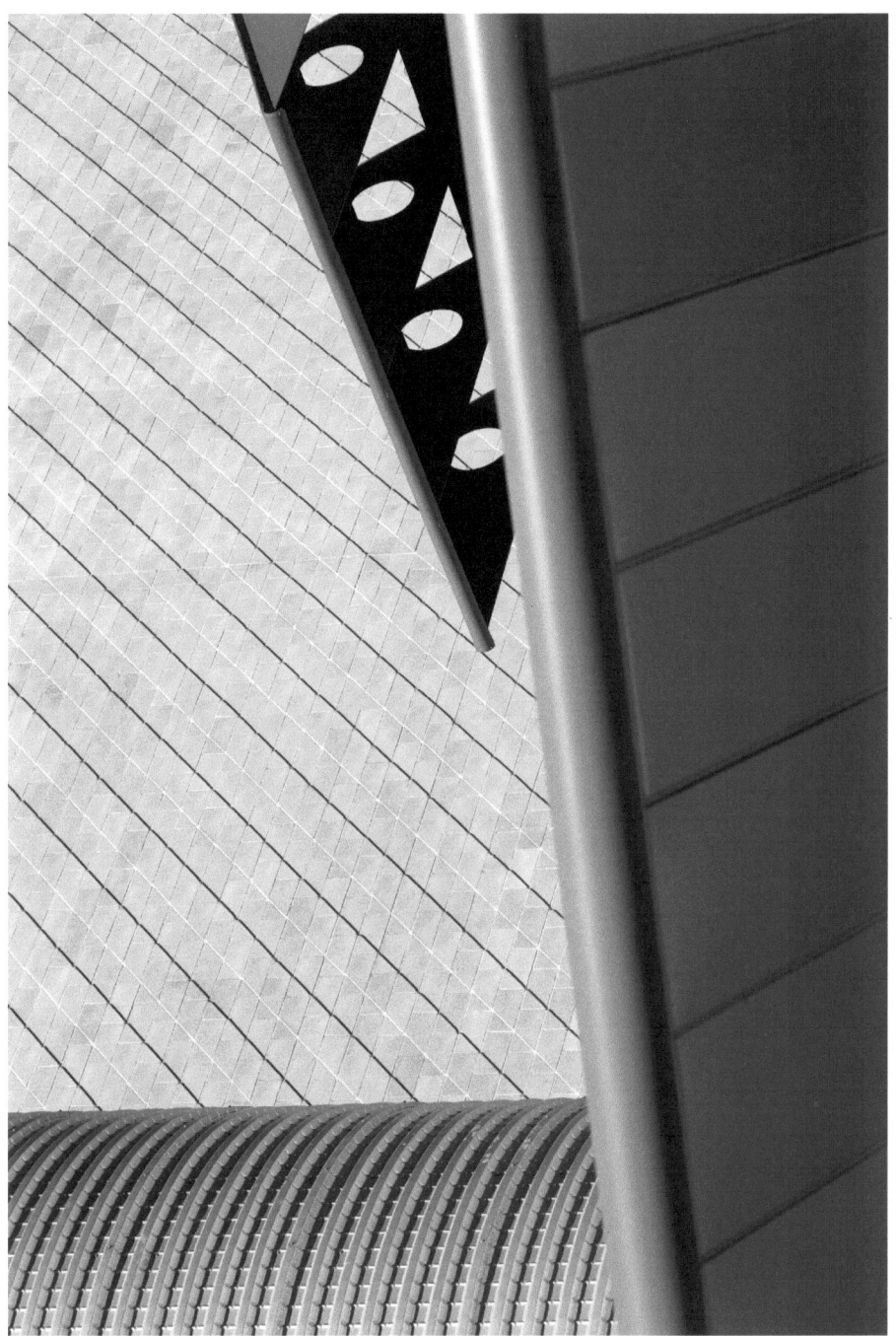

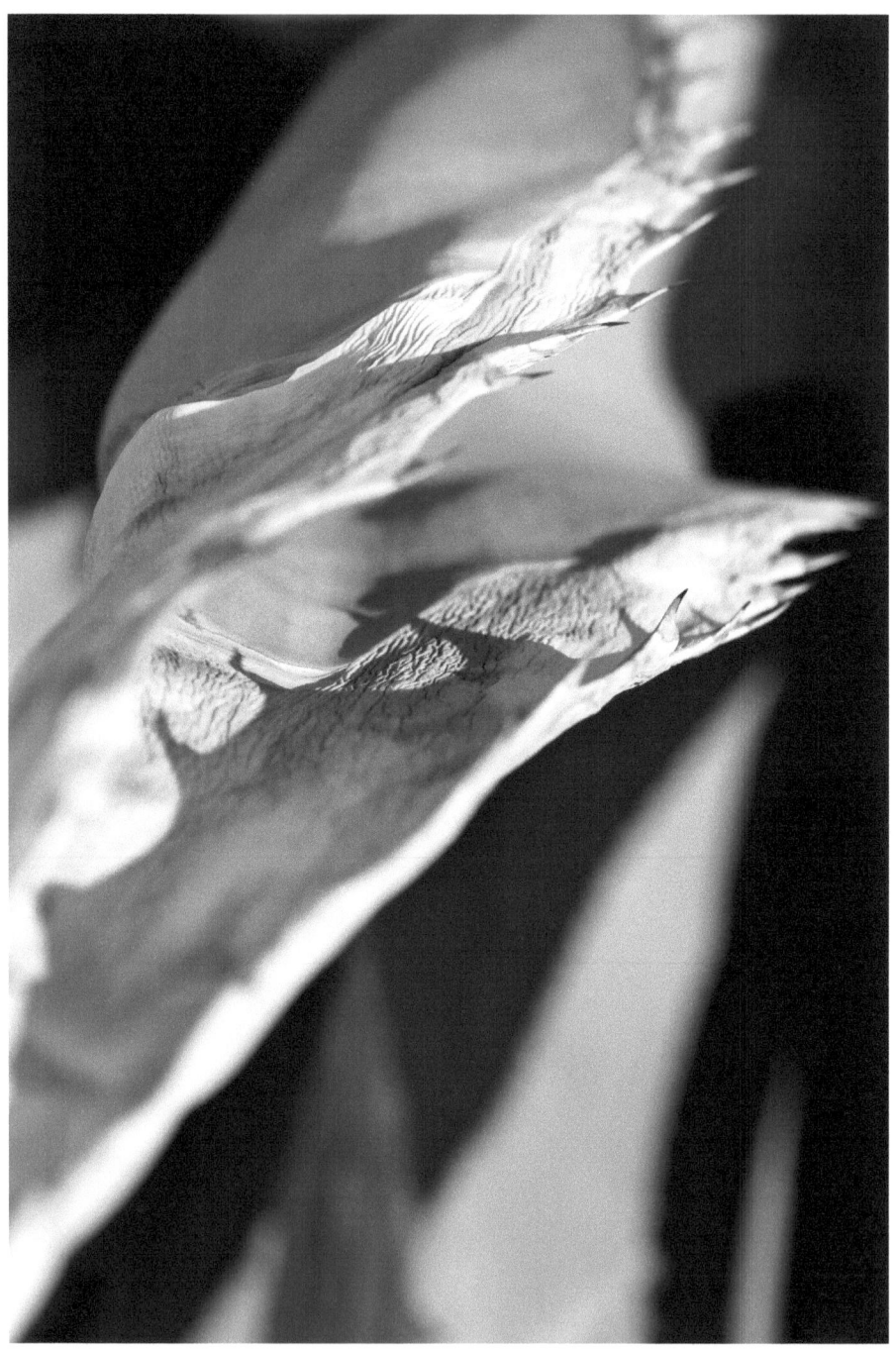

1581

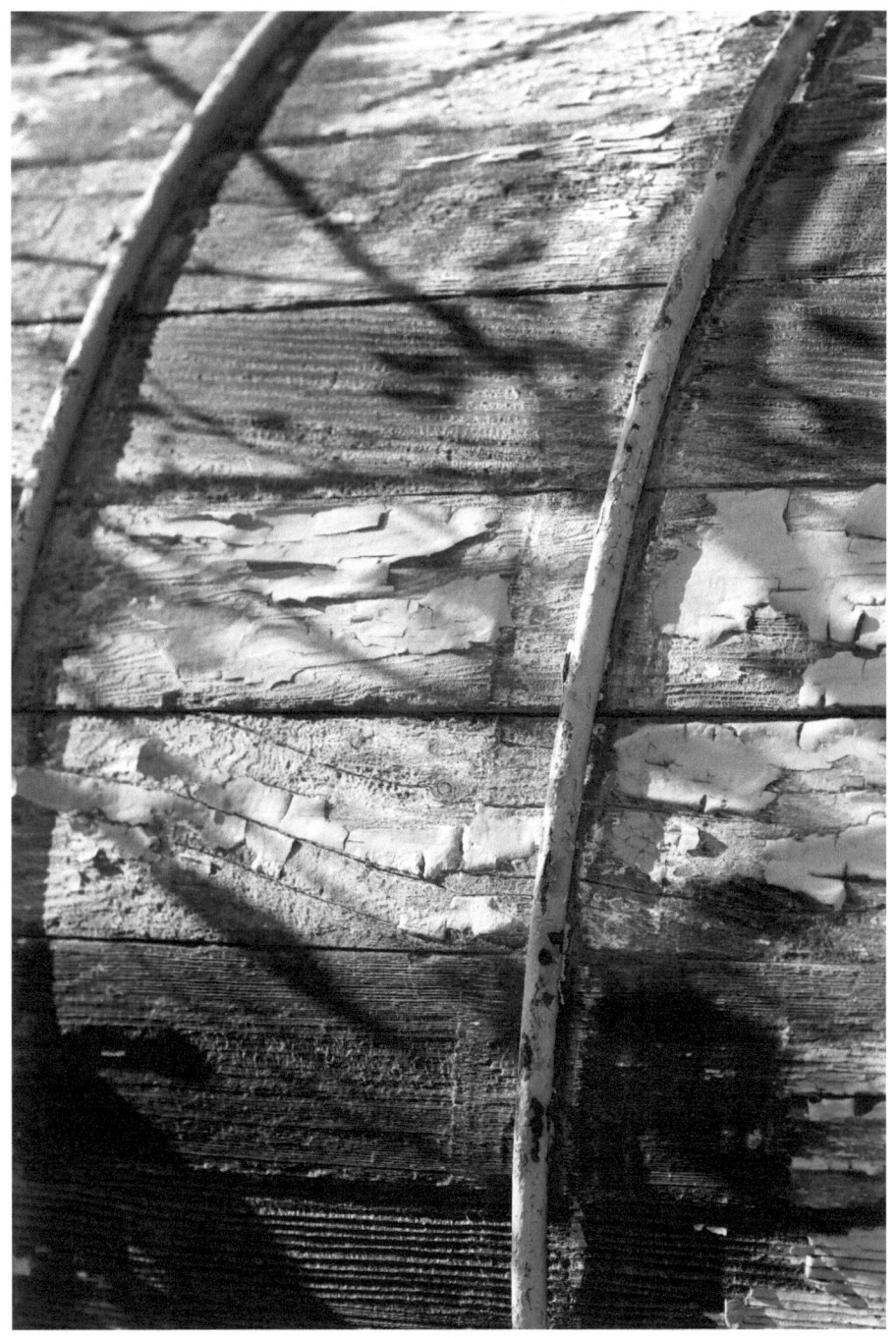

1608

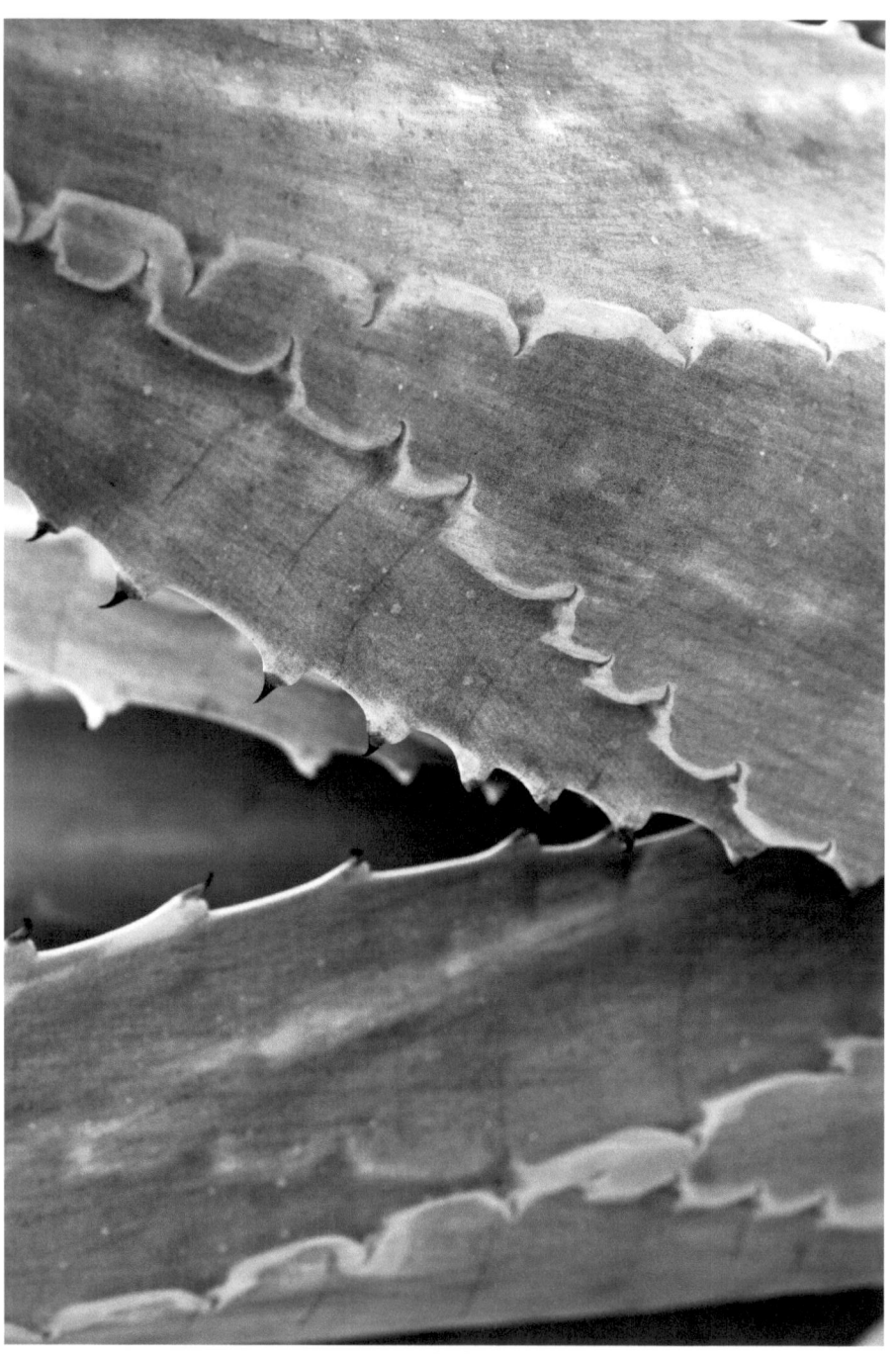

1976

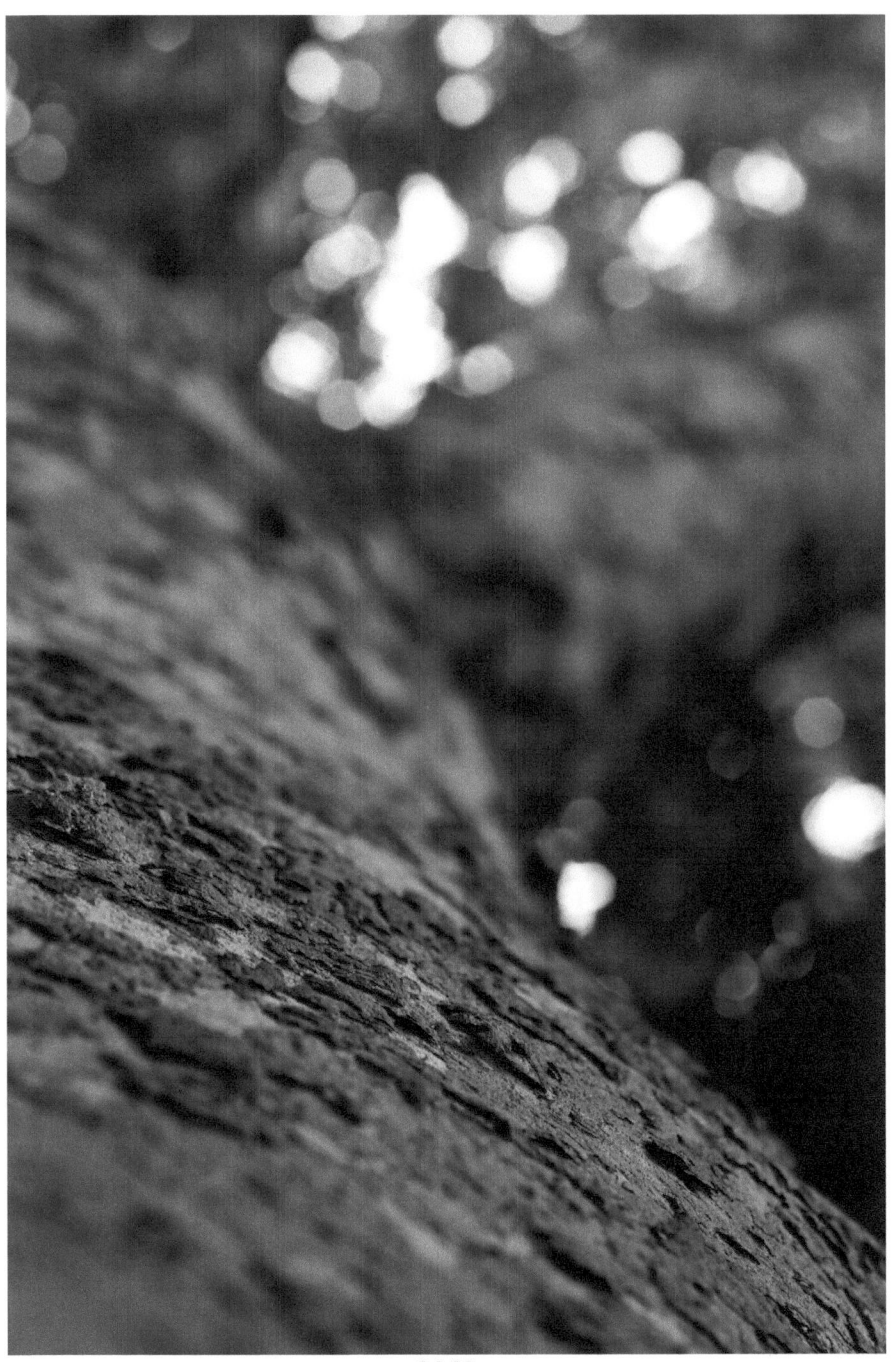

2068

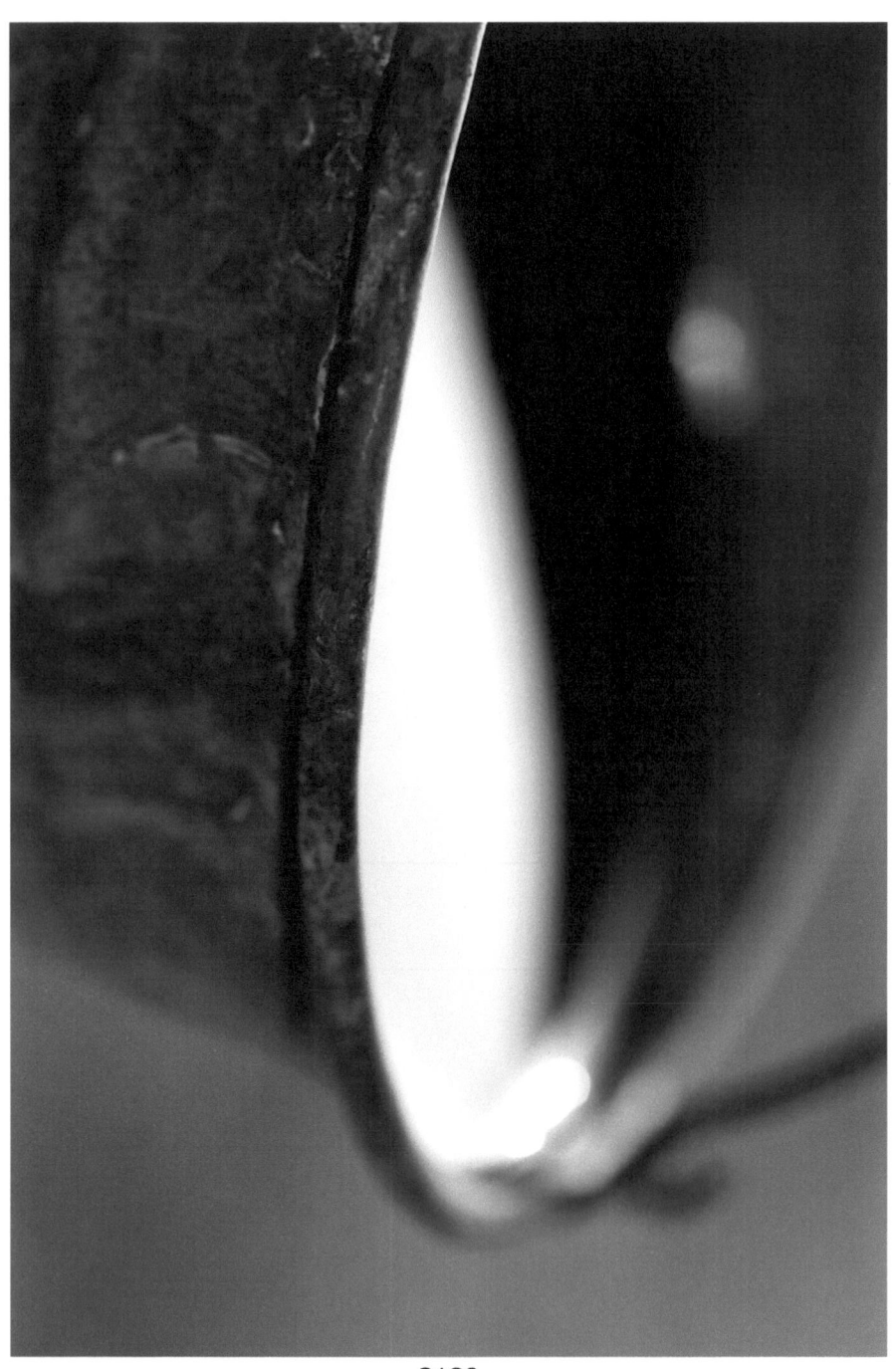

2180

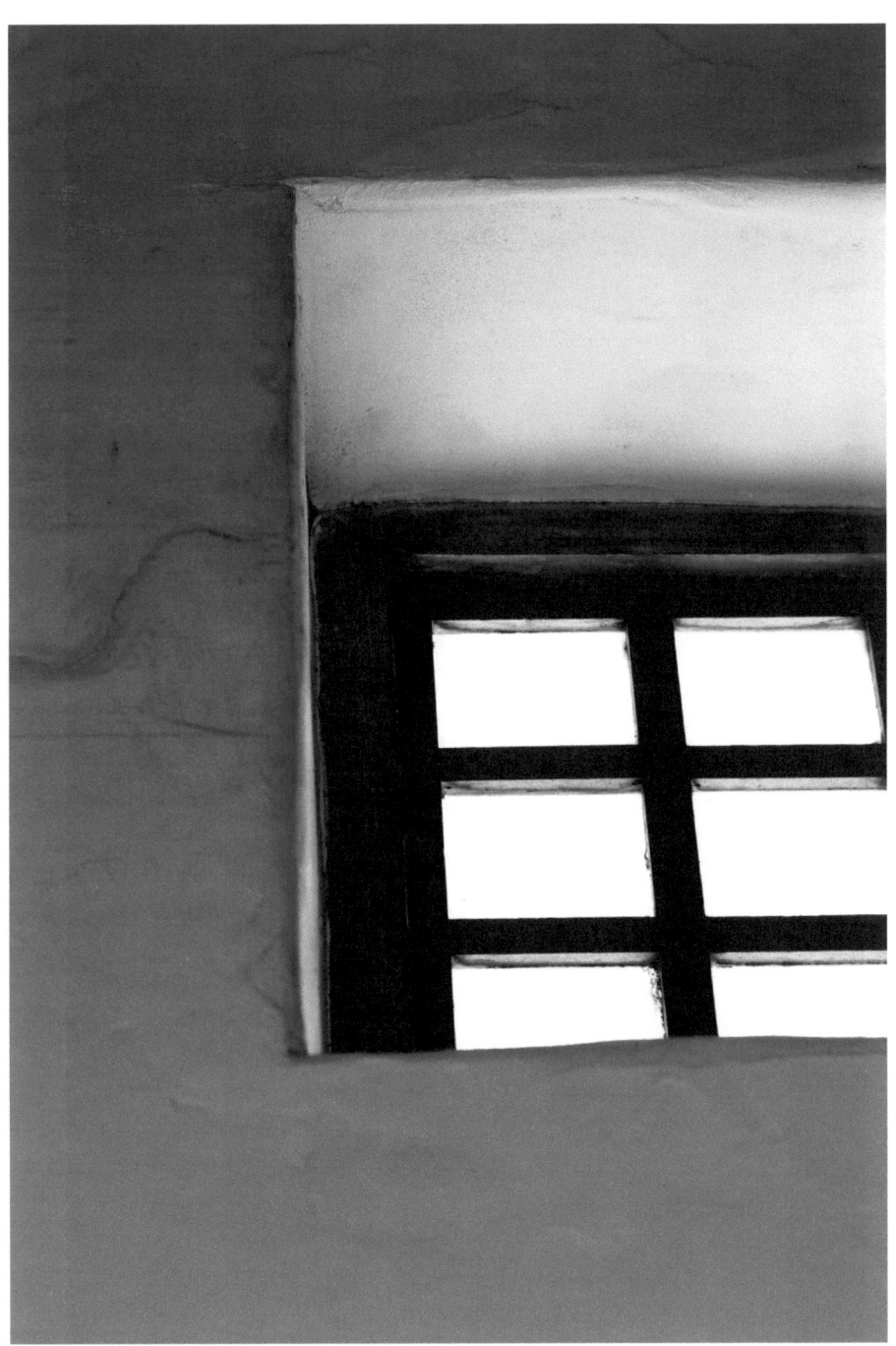

2397

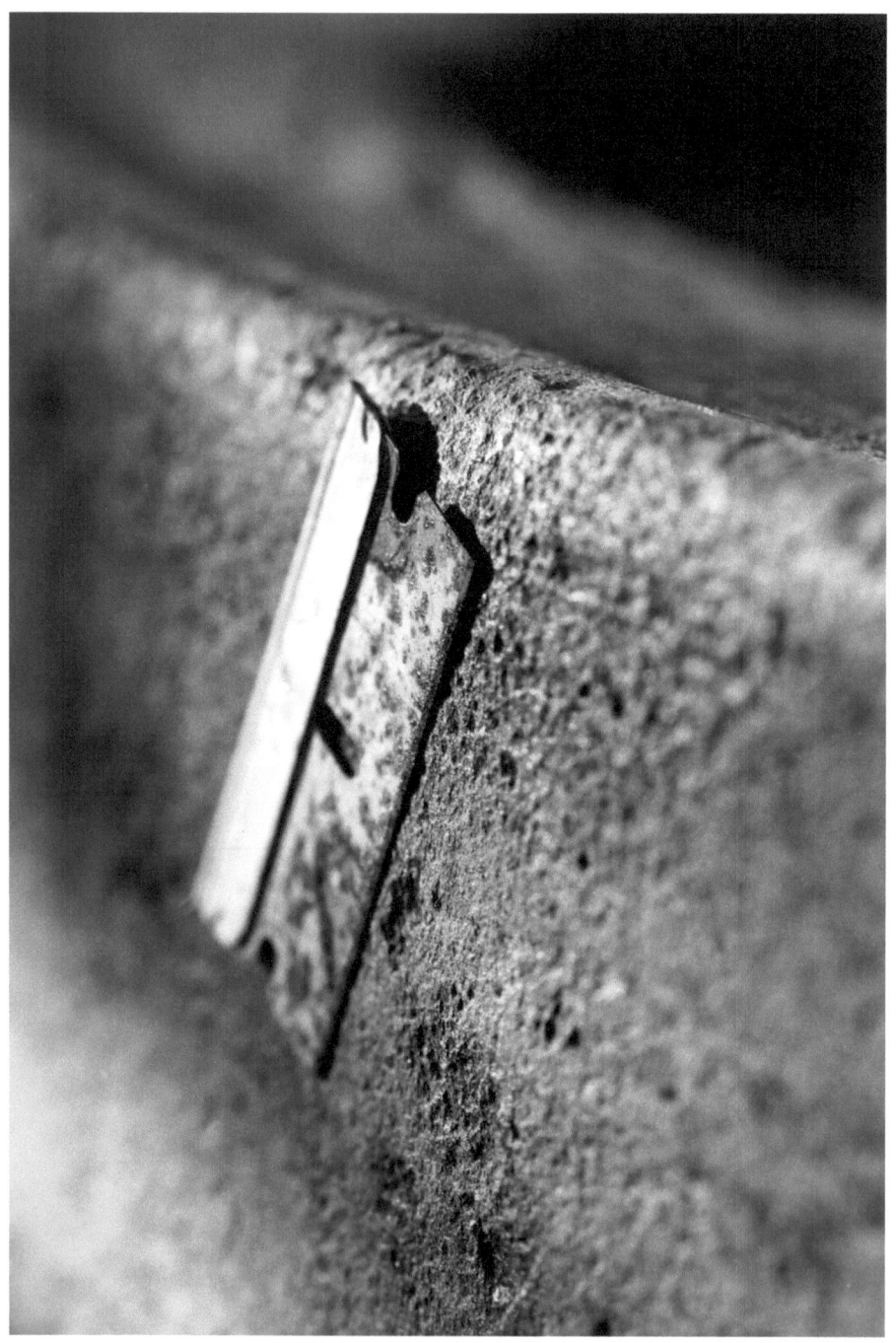

2467

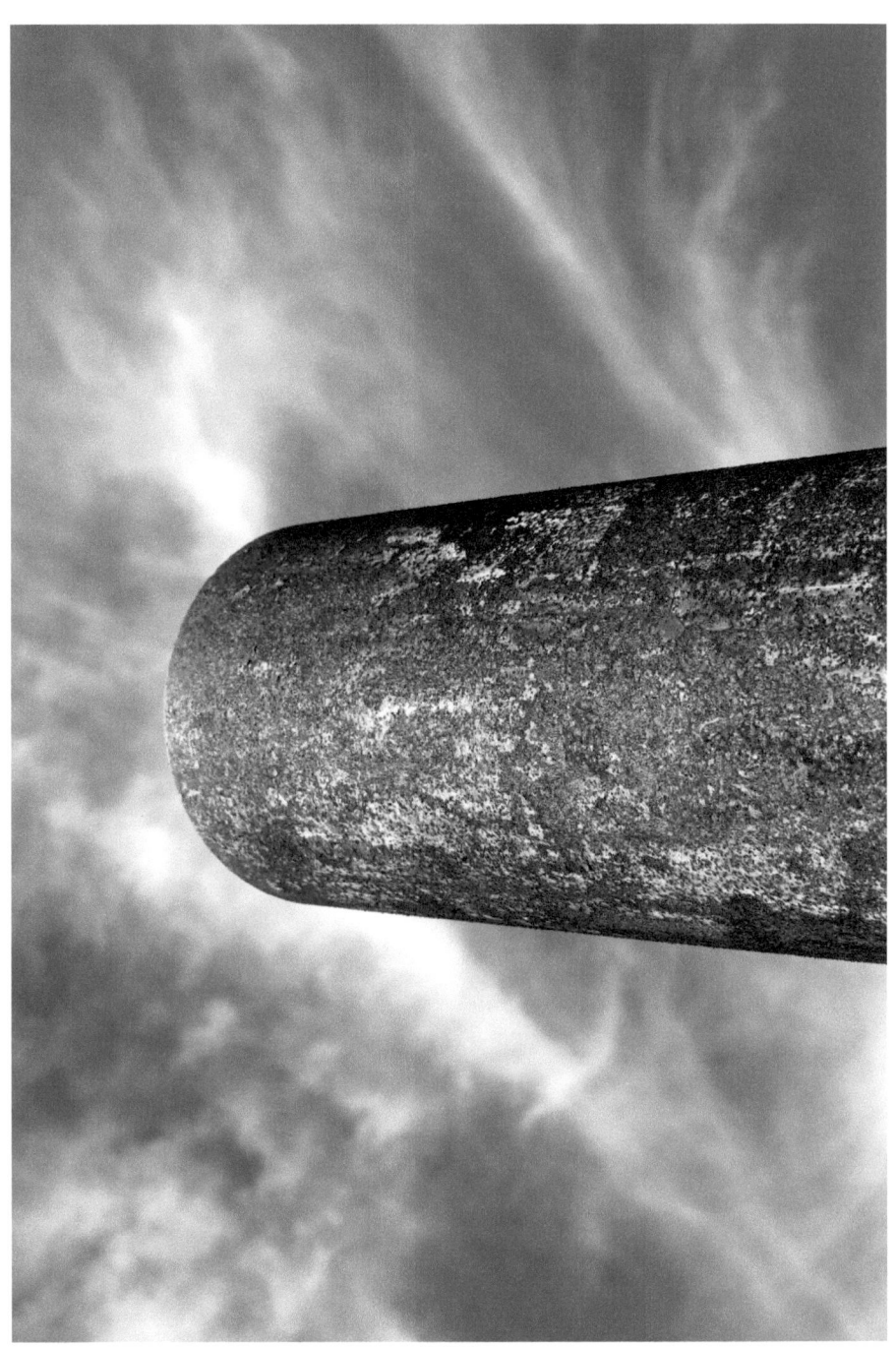

2495

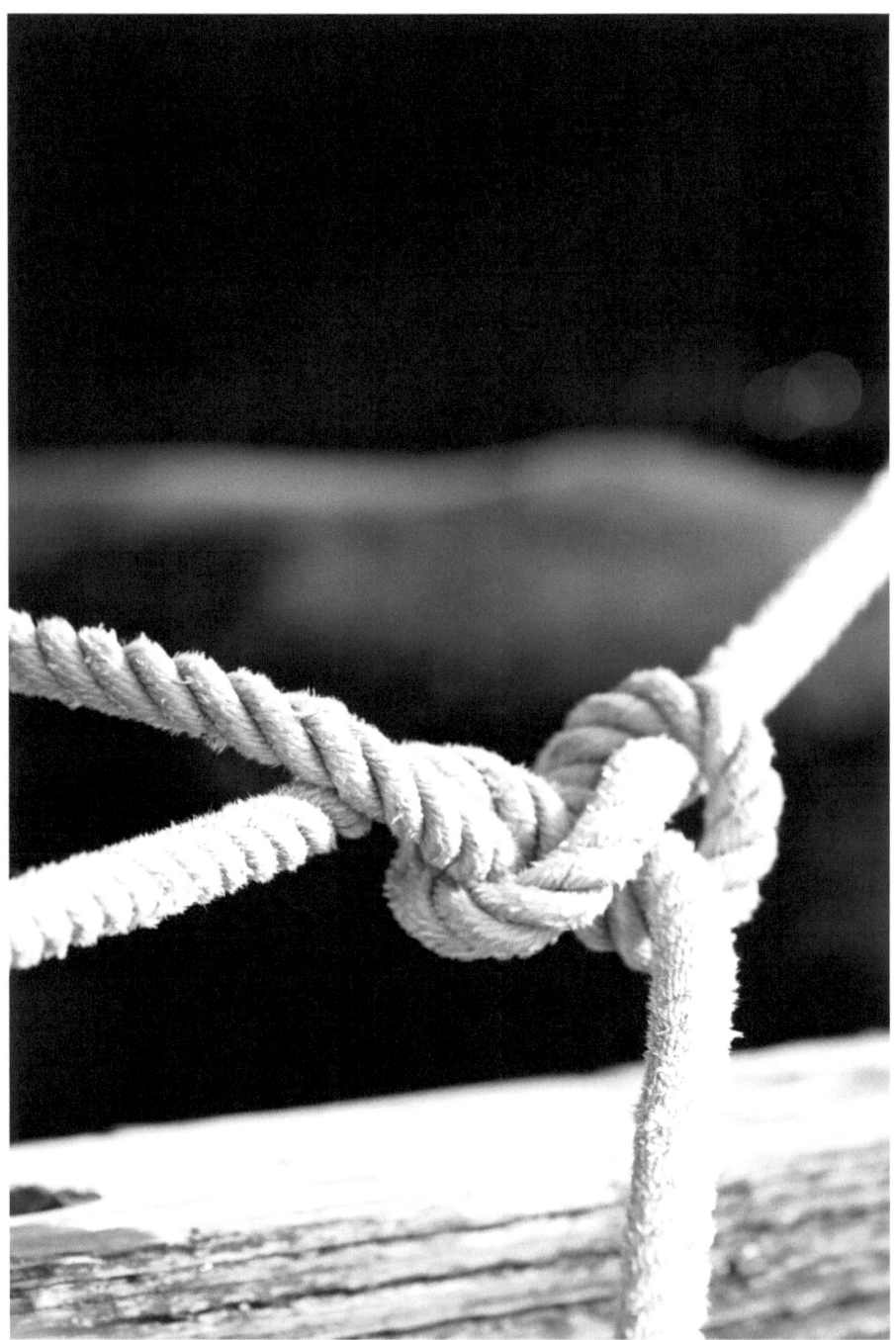

2686

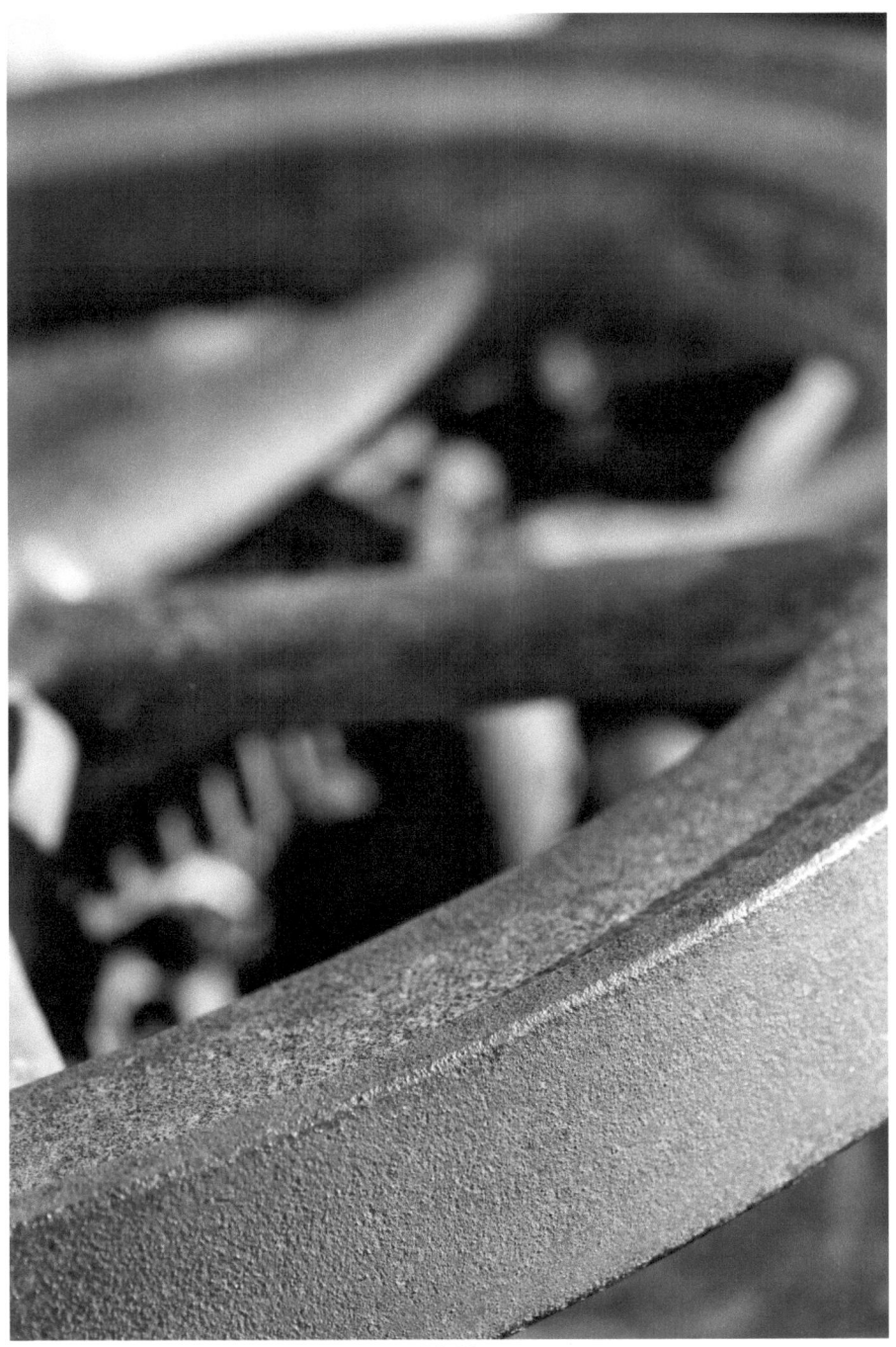

2962

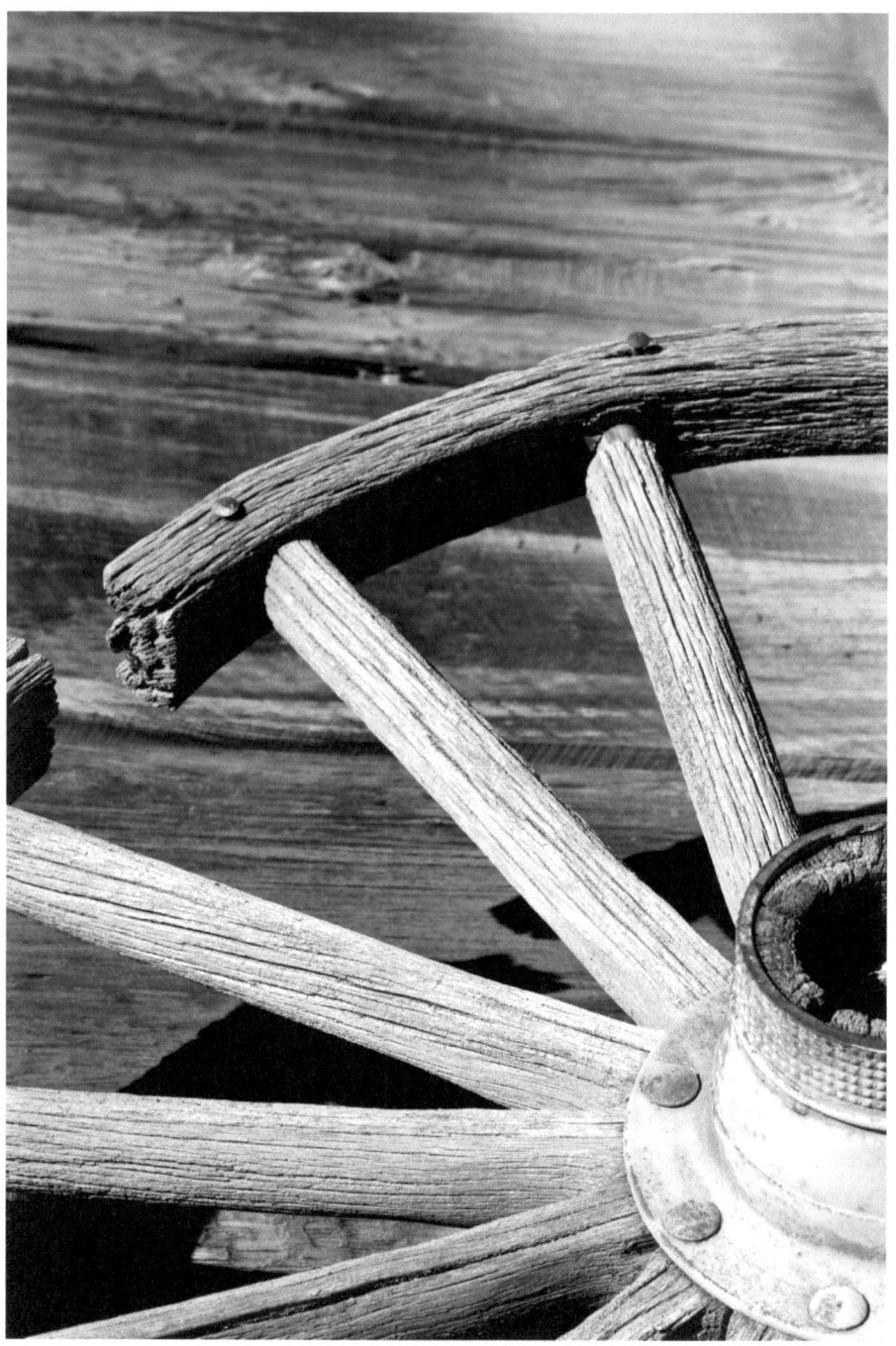

3147

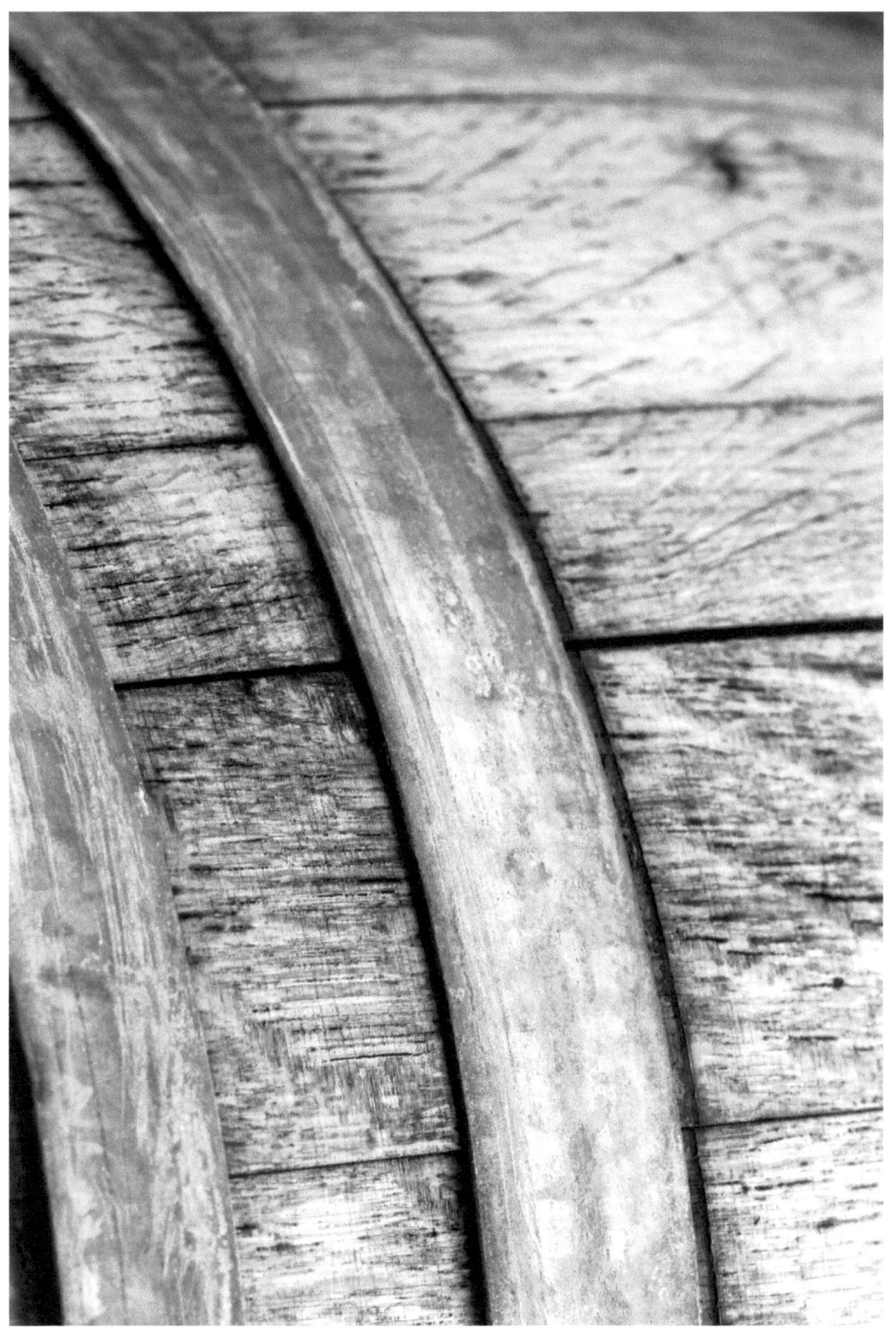

3151

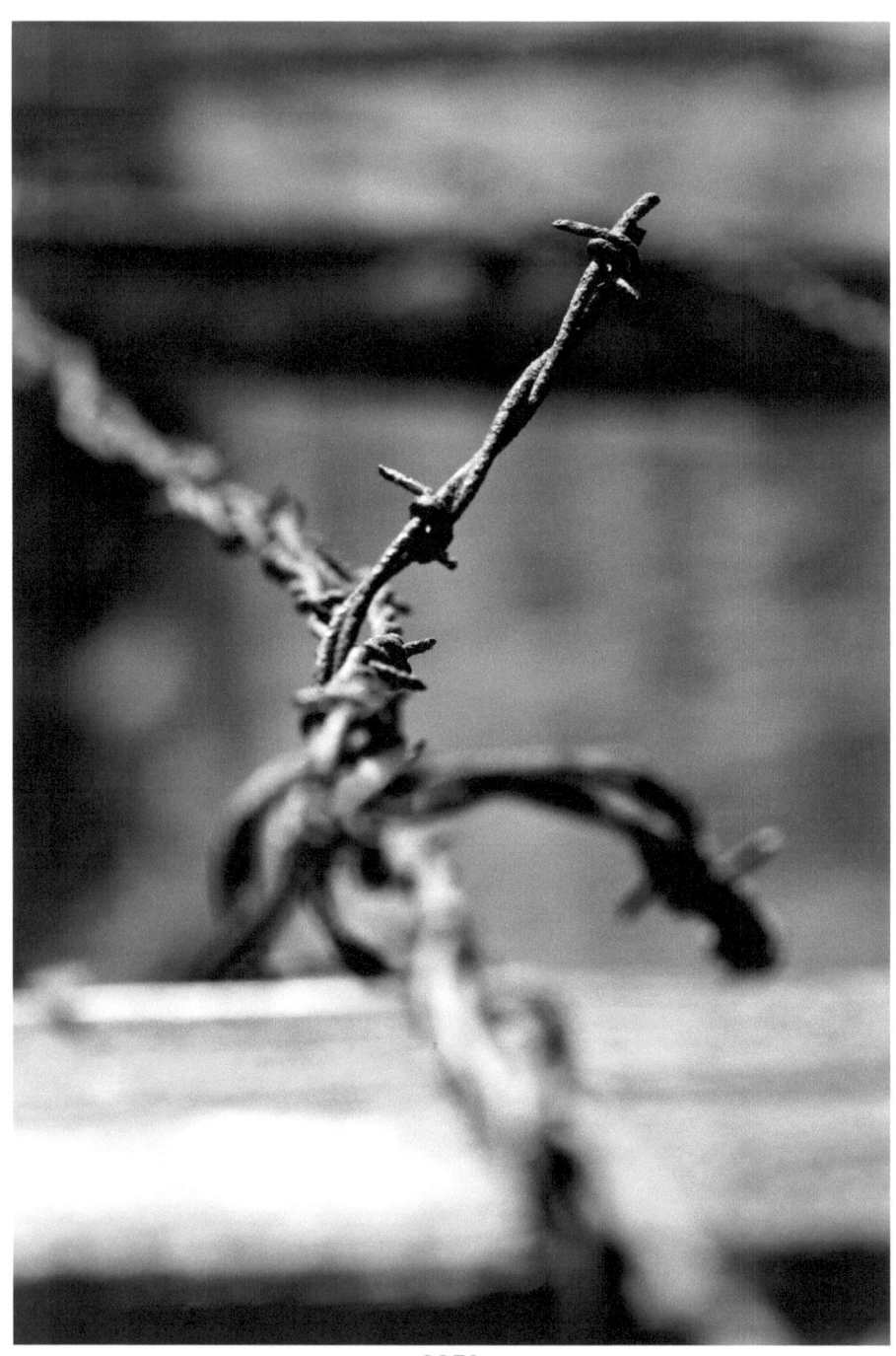

3359

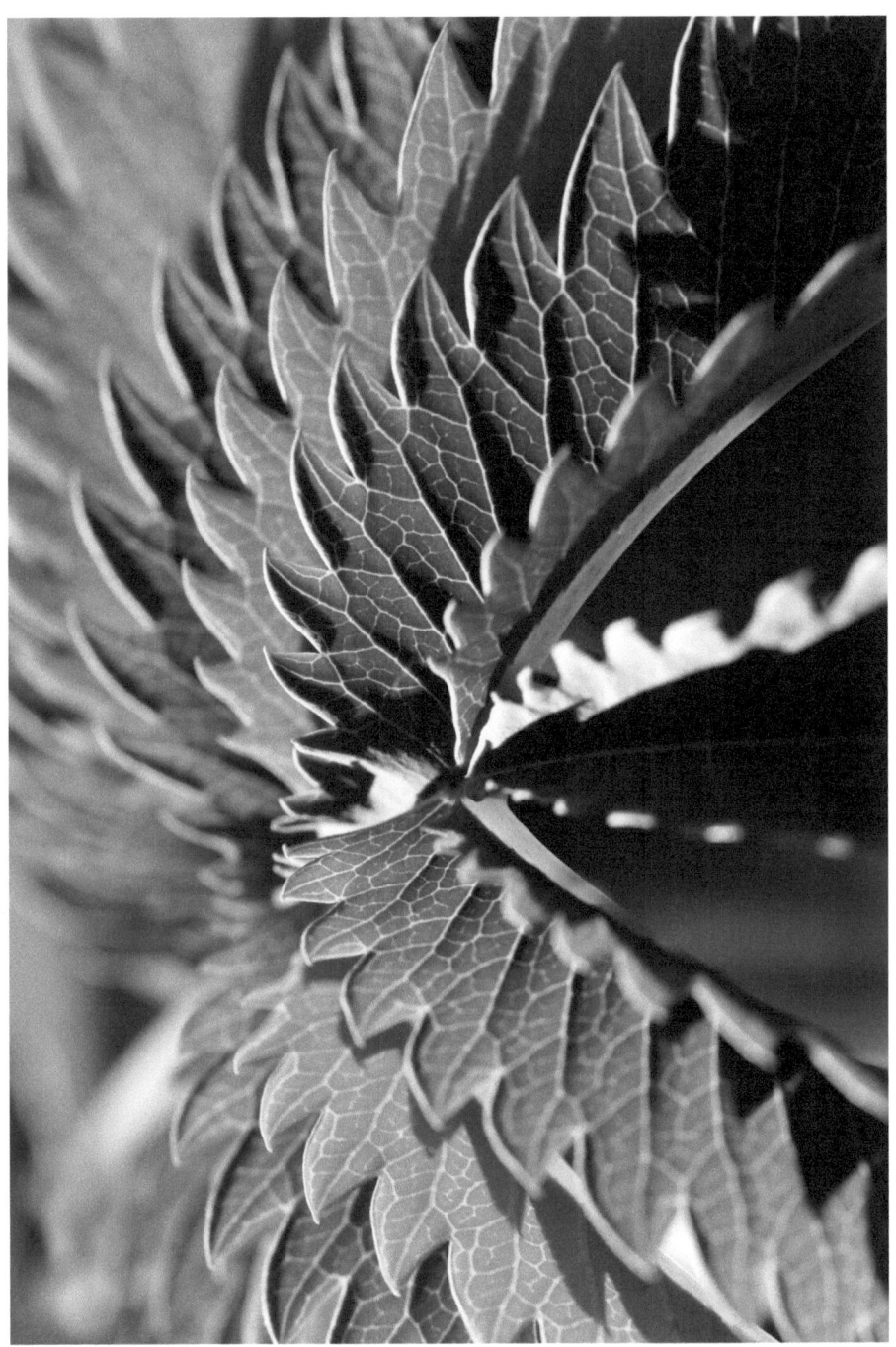

3714

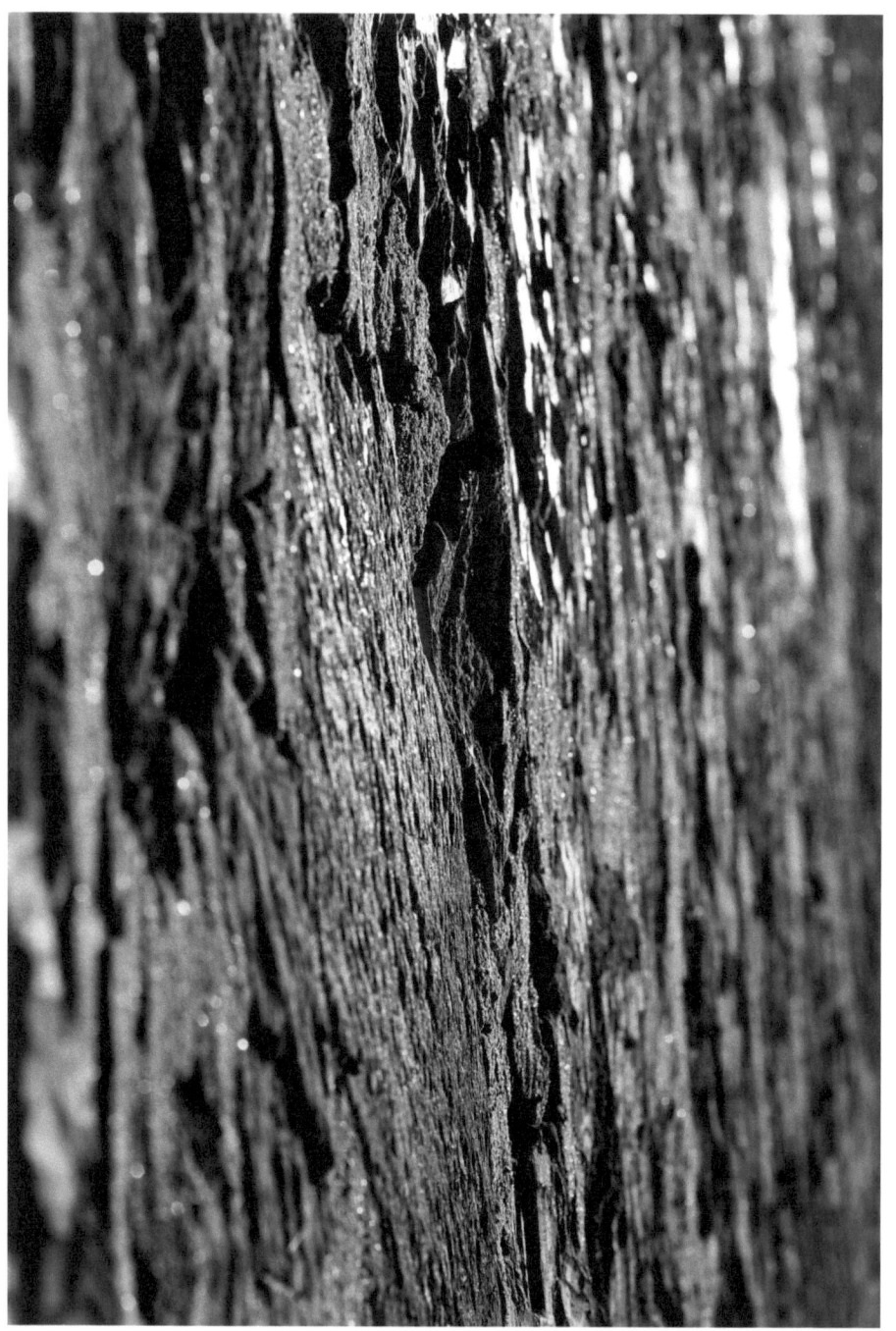

3881

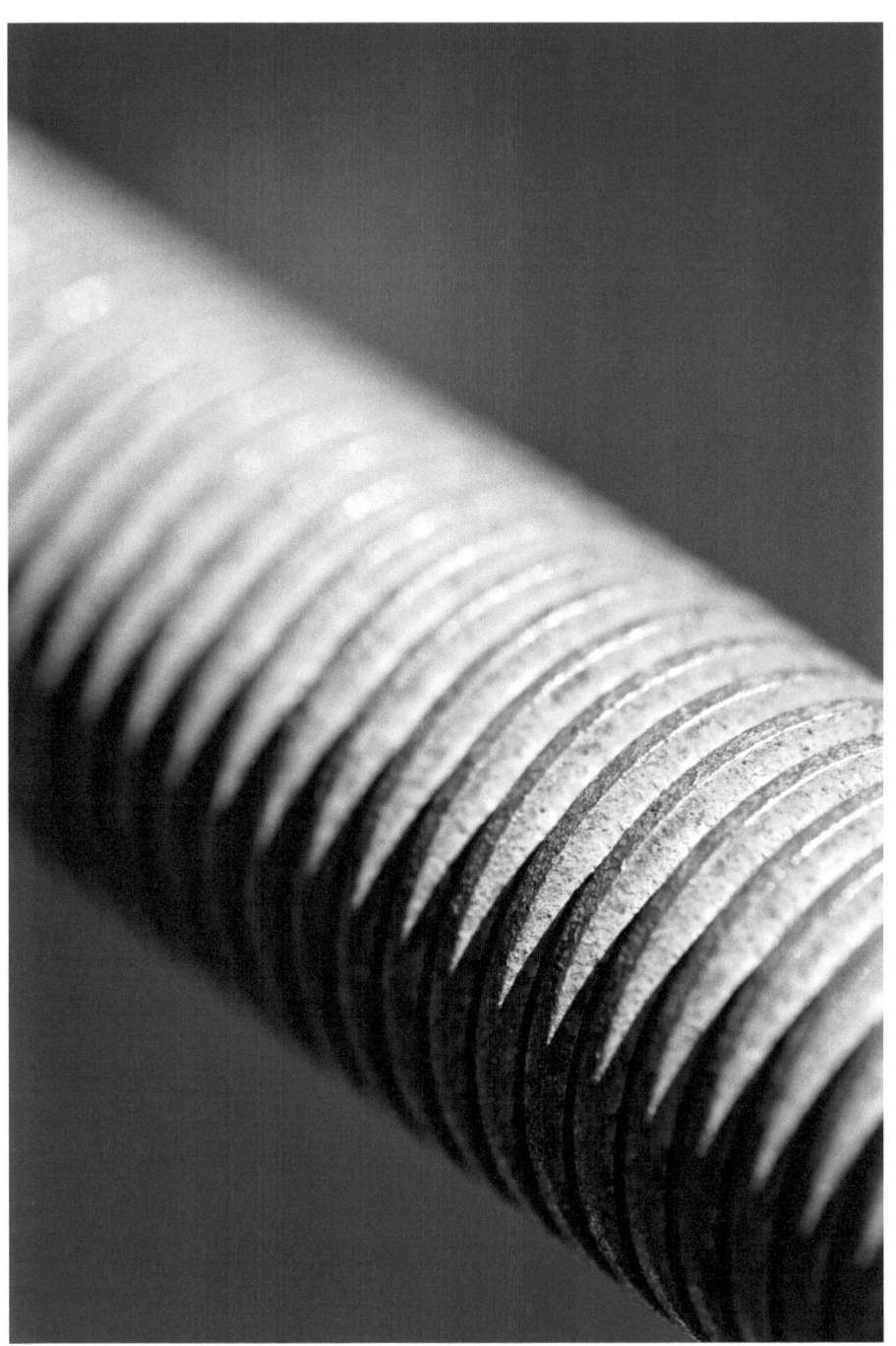

3937

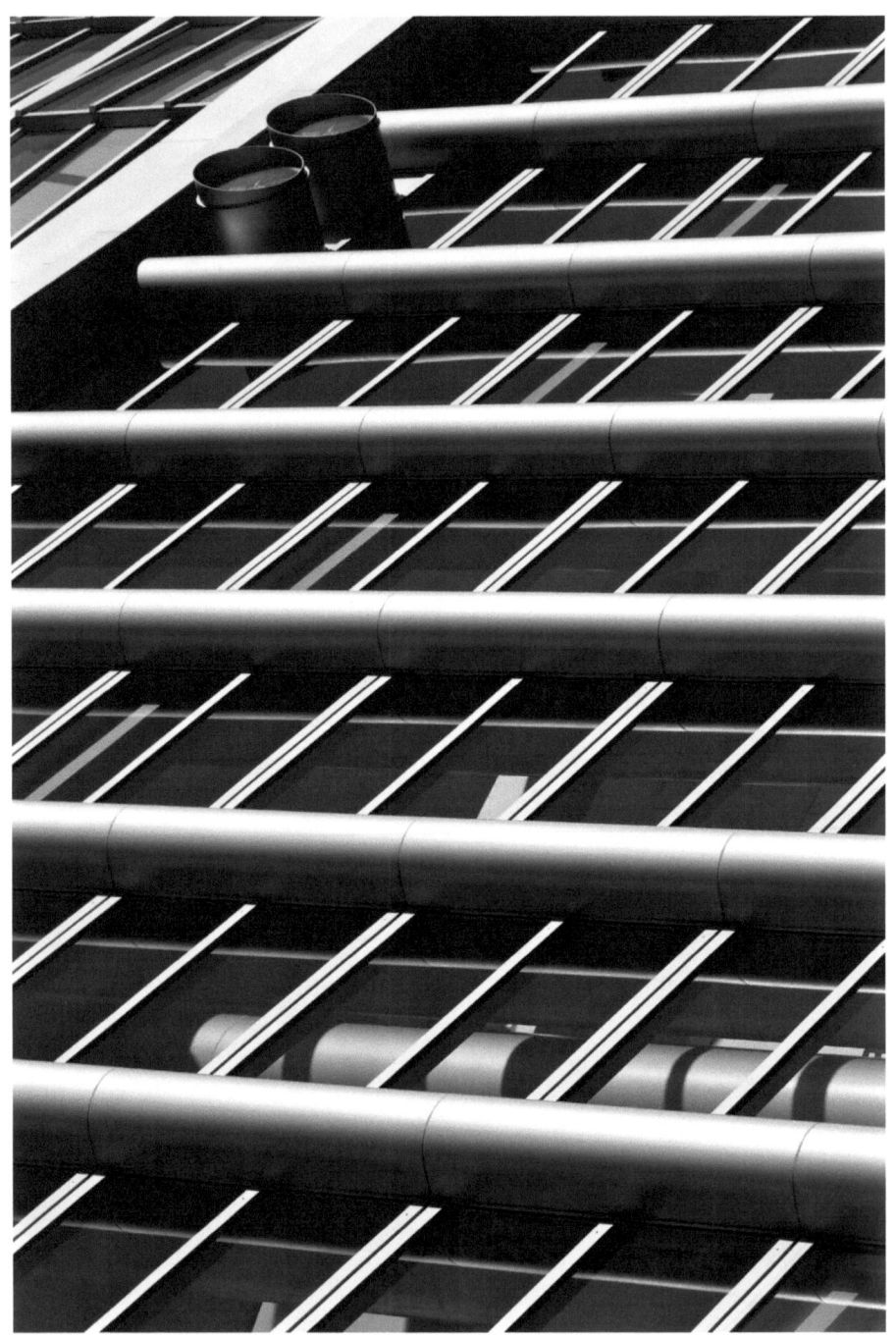

3943

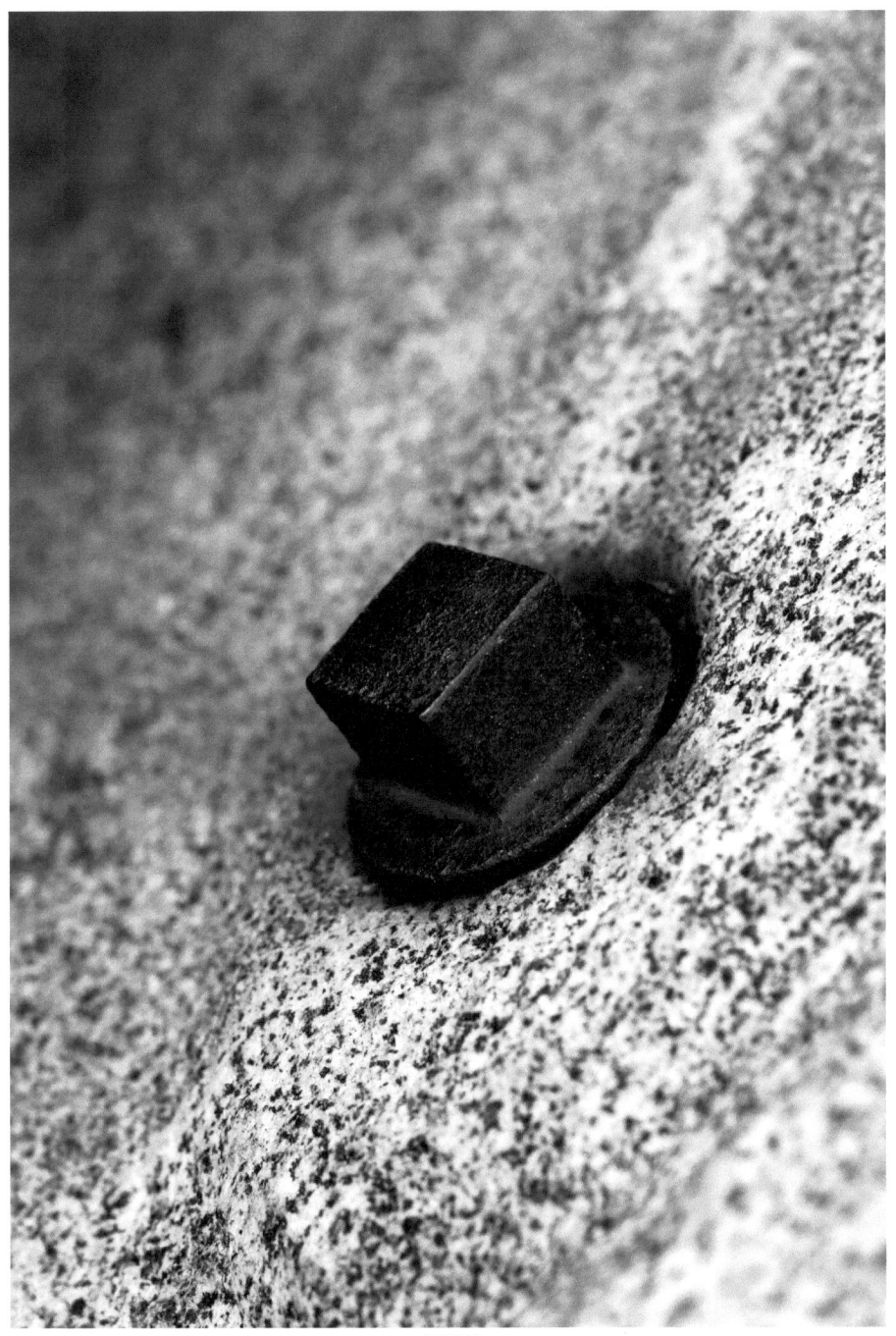

4035

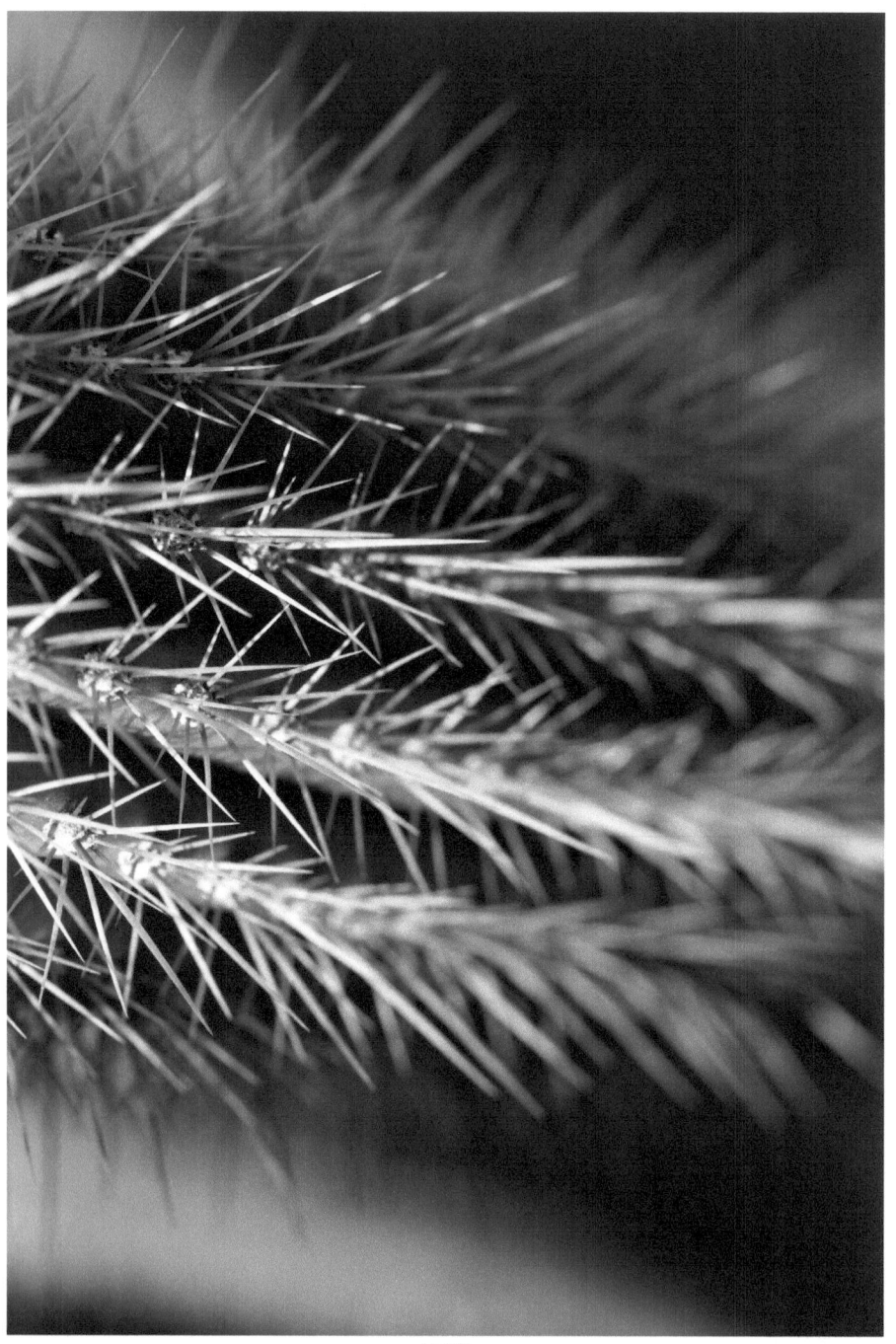

4070

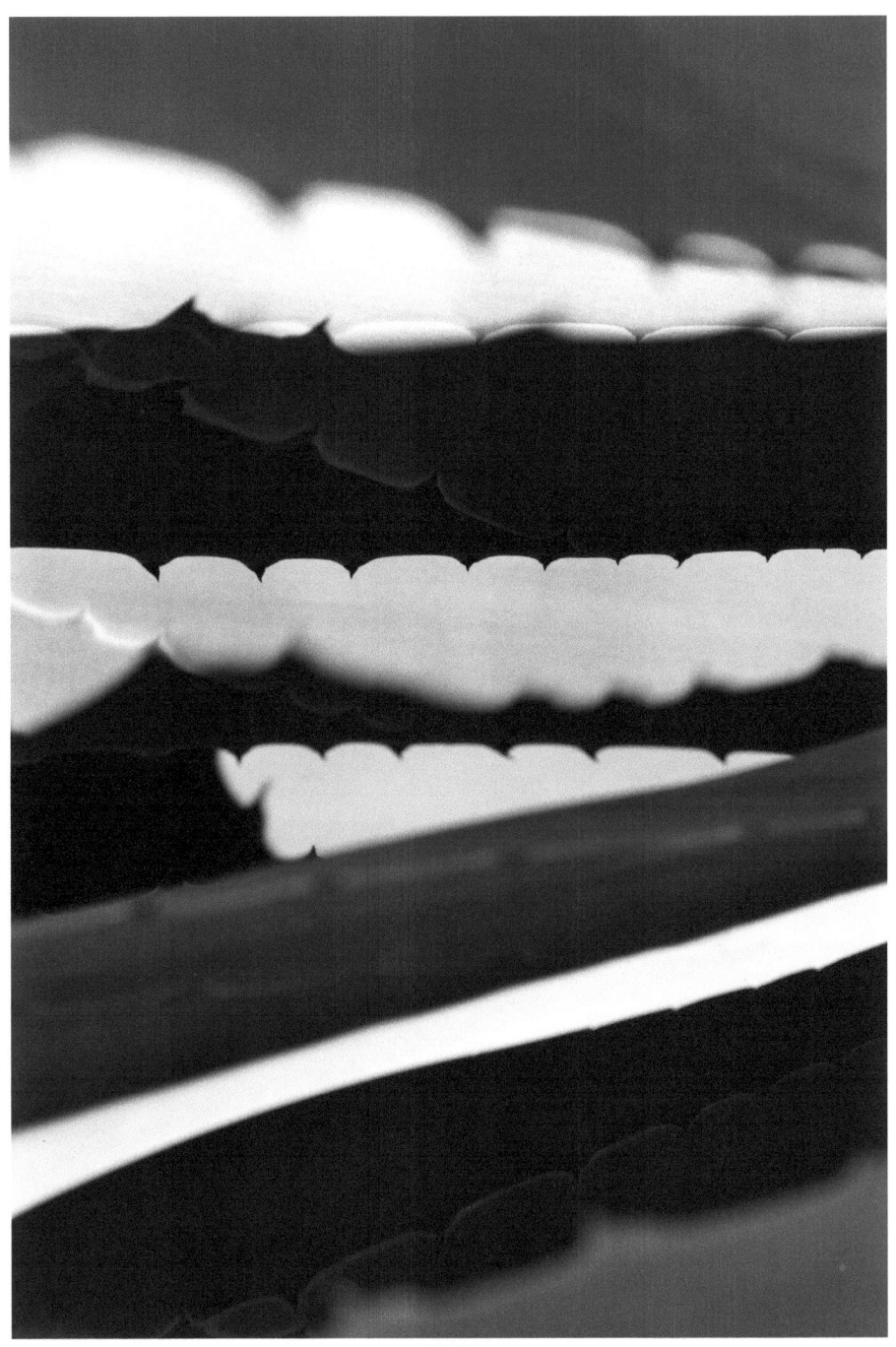

4099

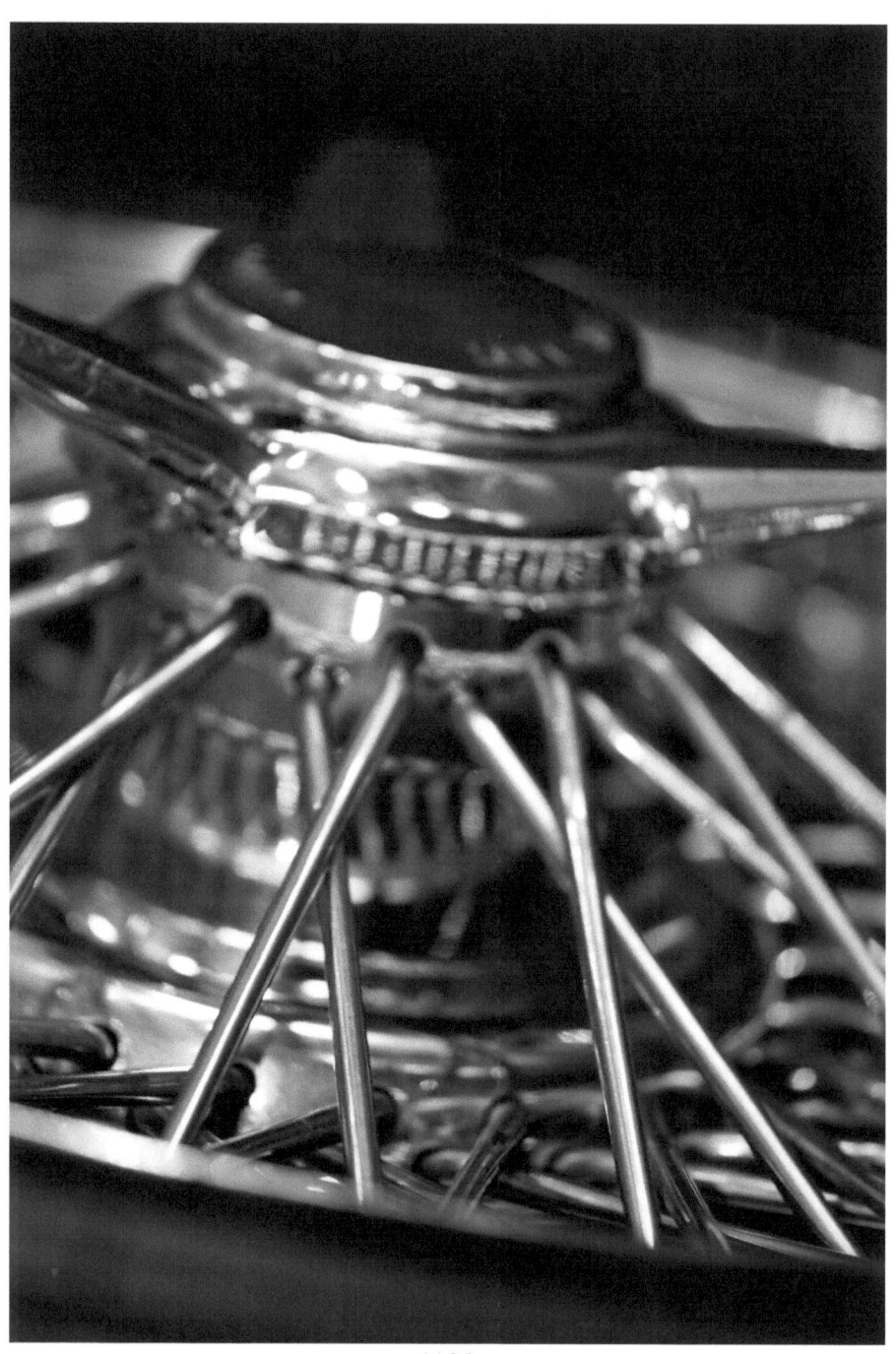

4193

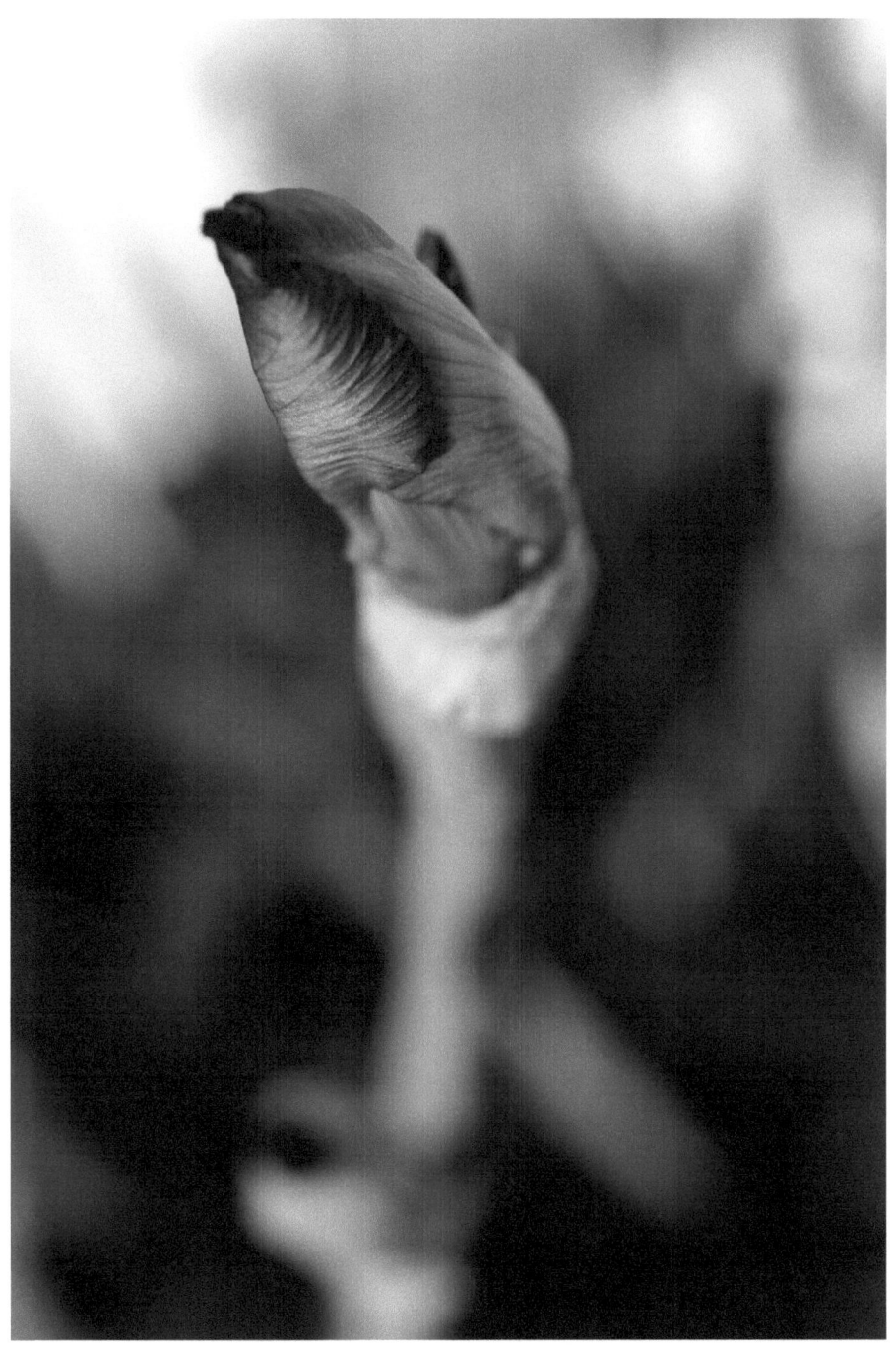

5492

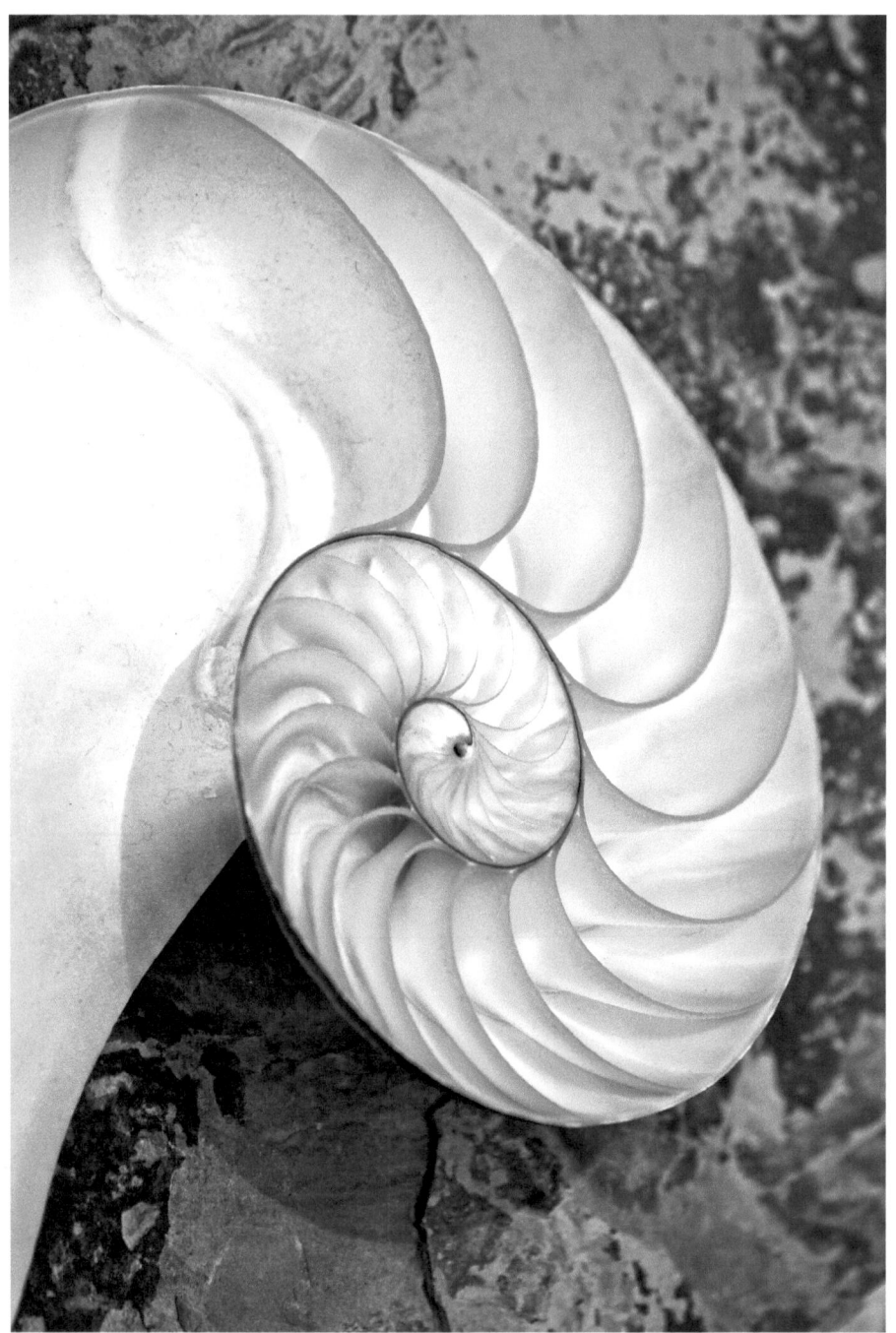

5708

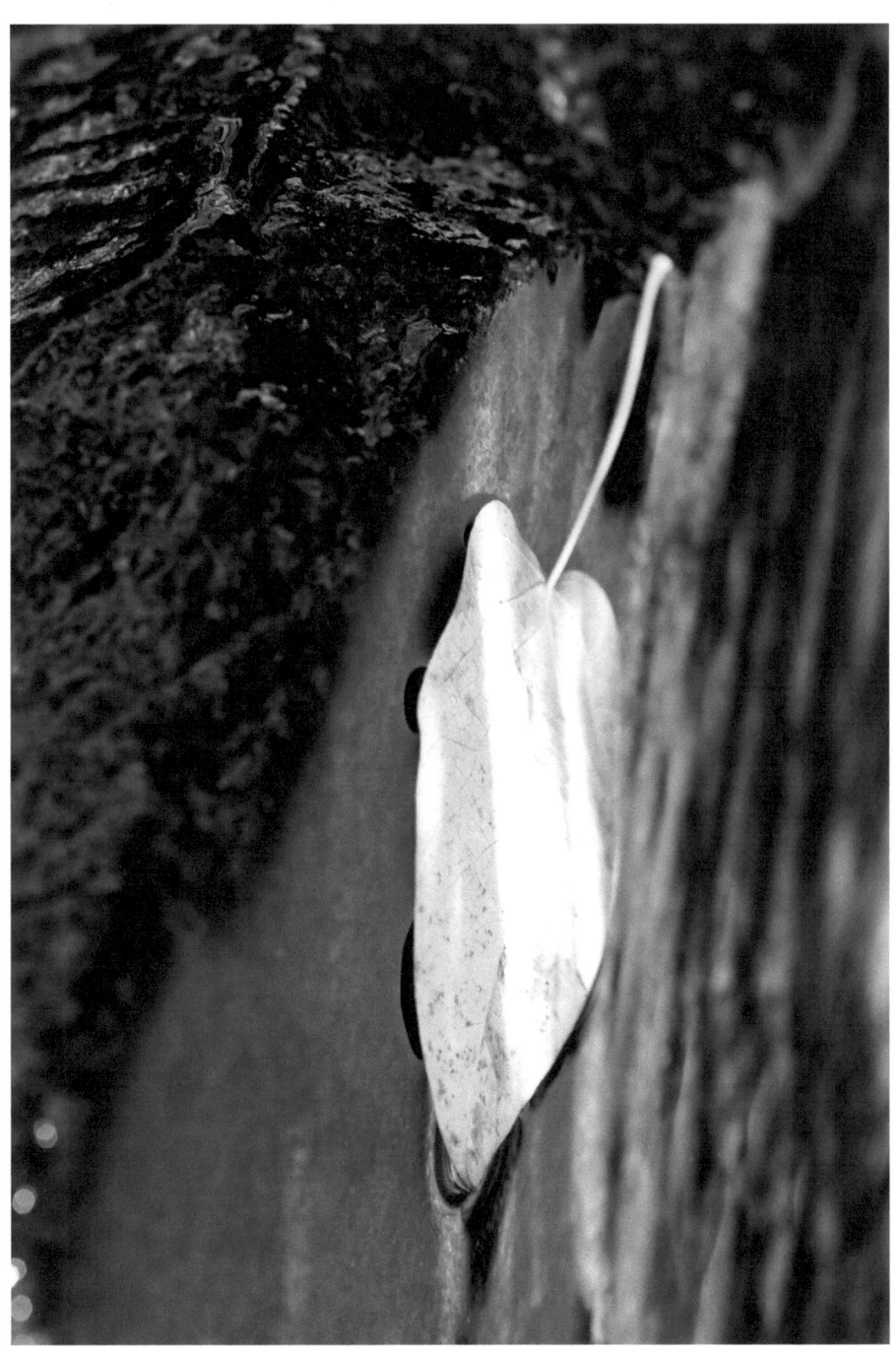

5750

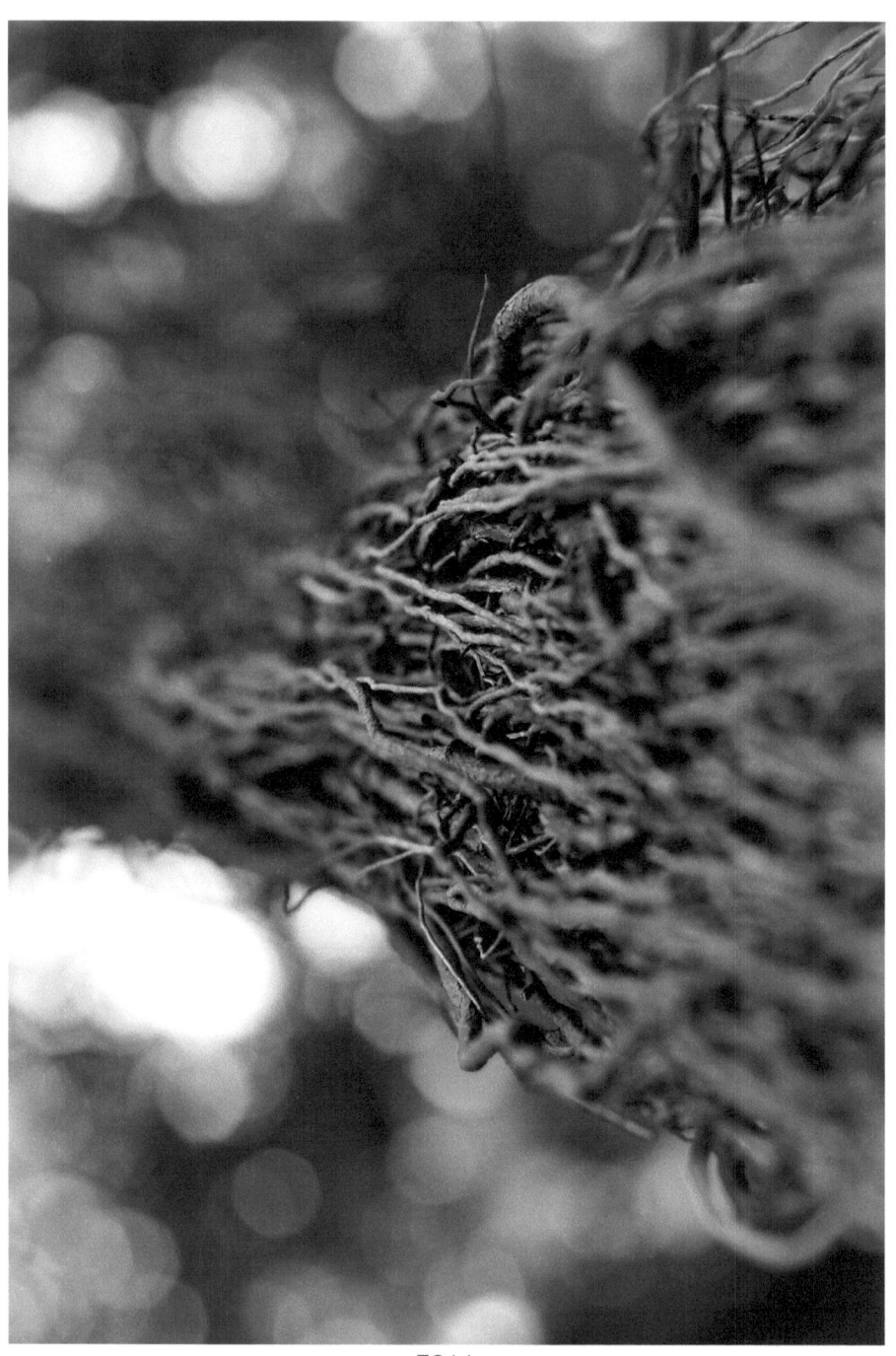

5811

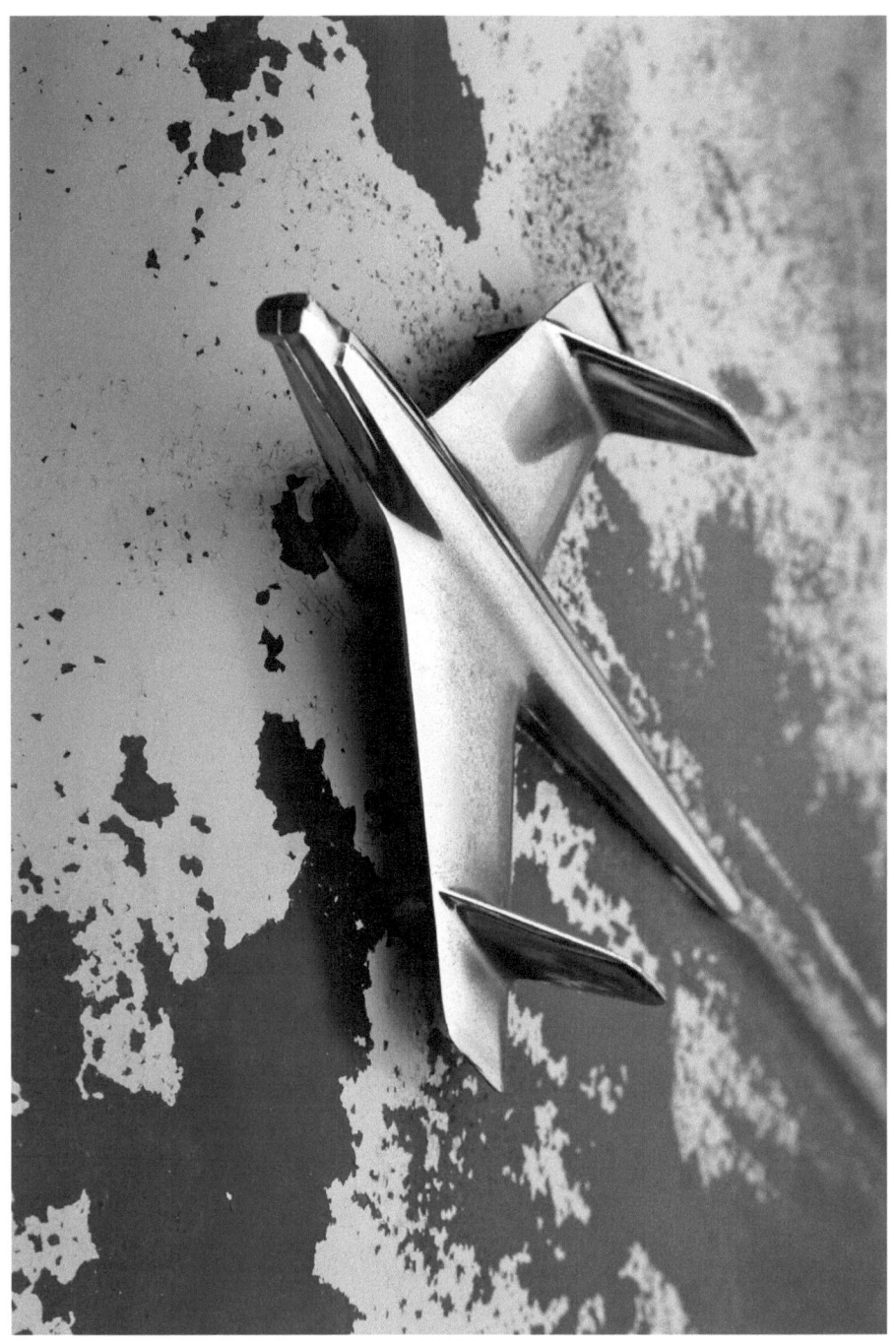

5846

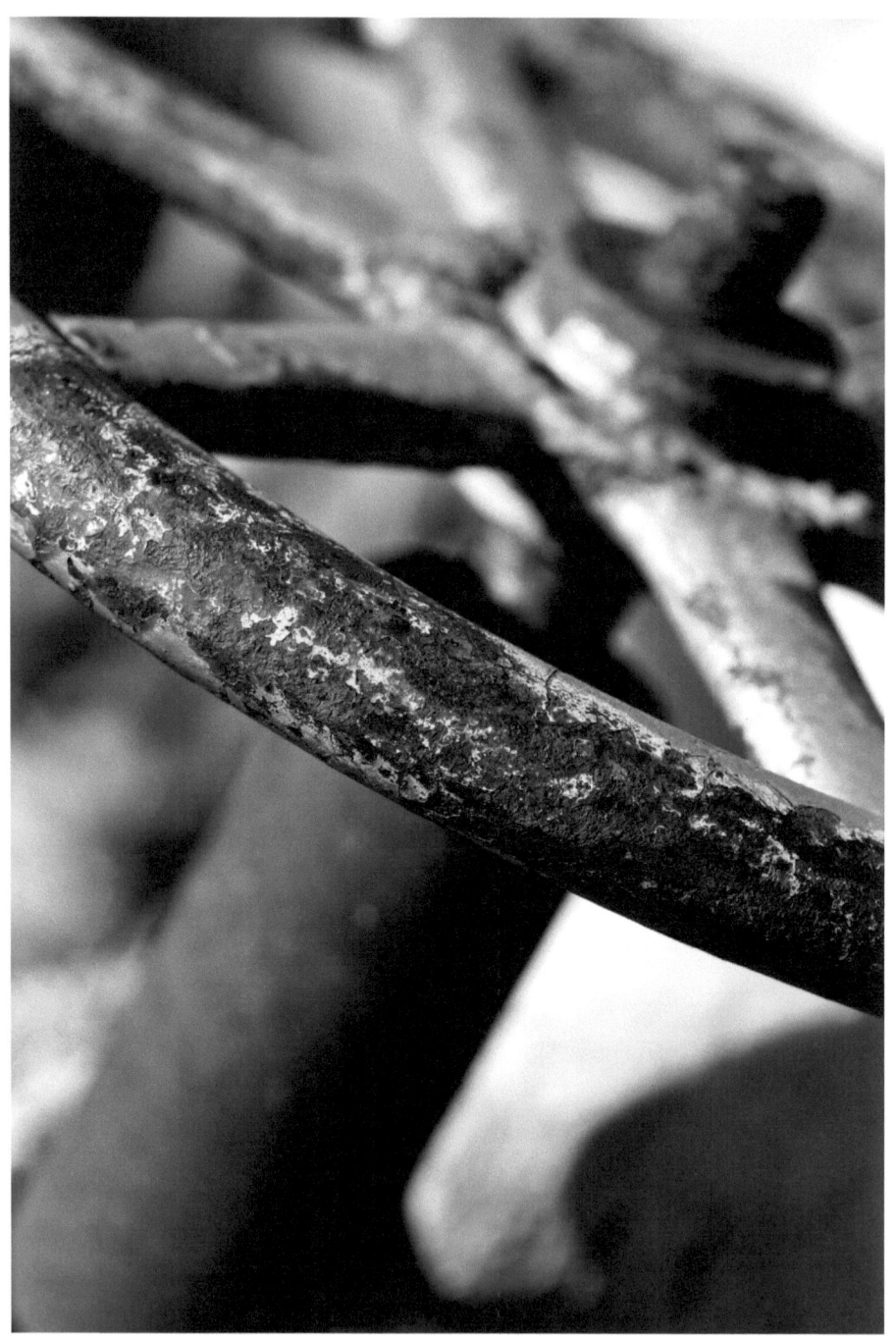

6095

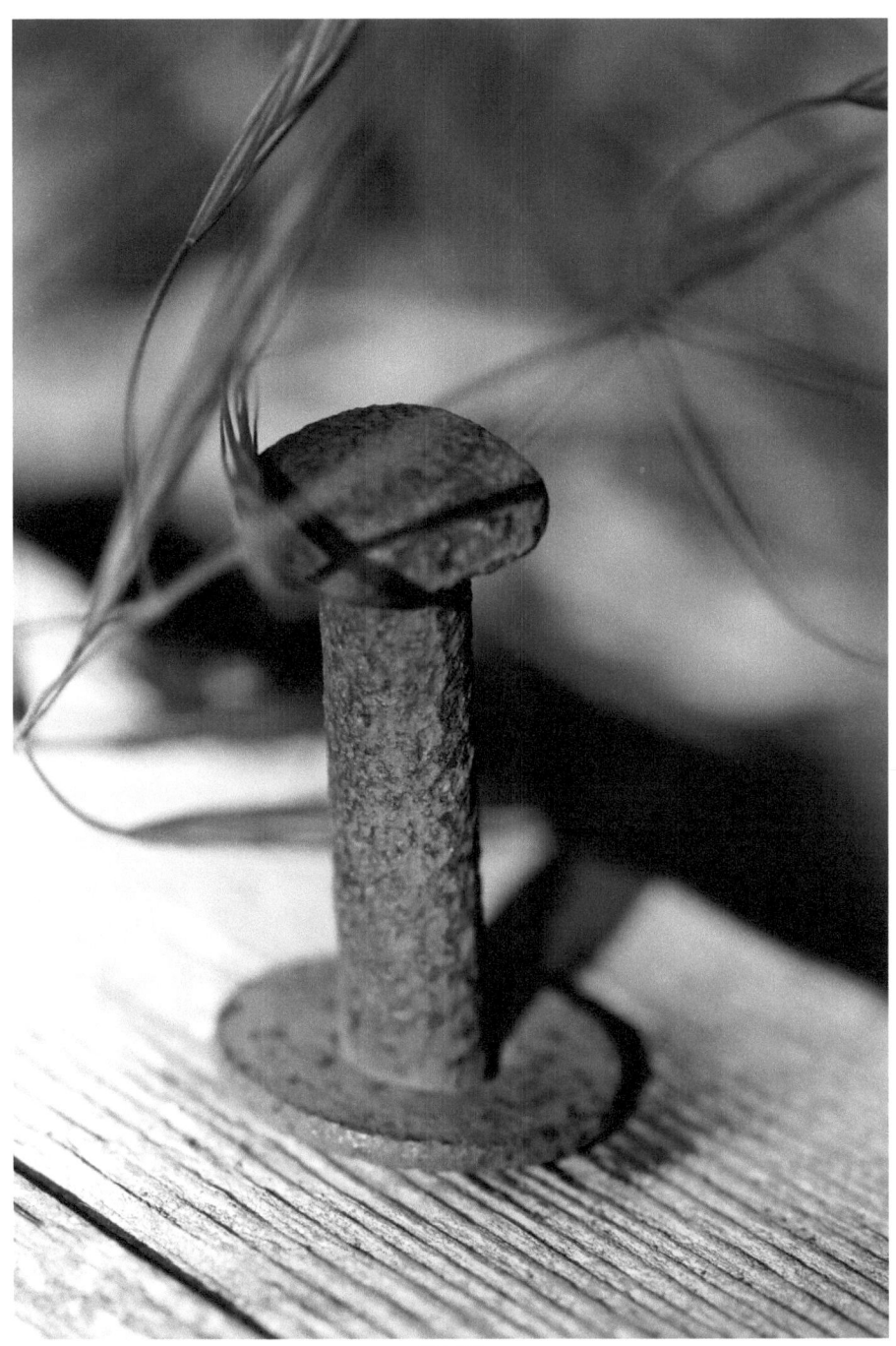

7182

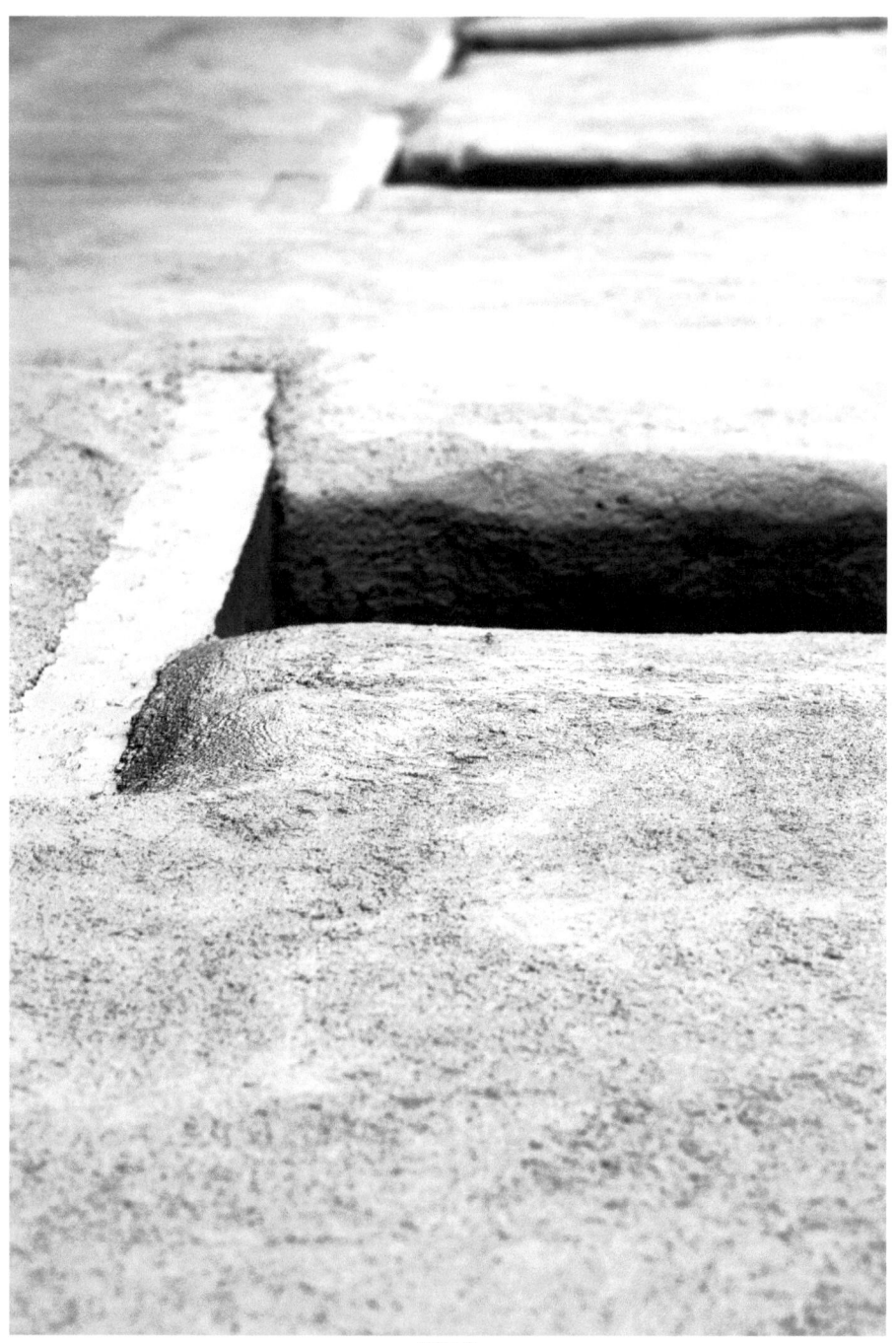

7843

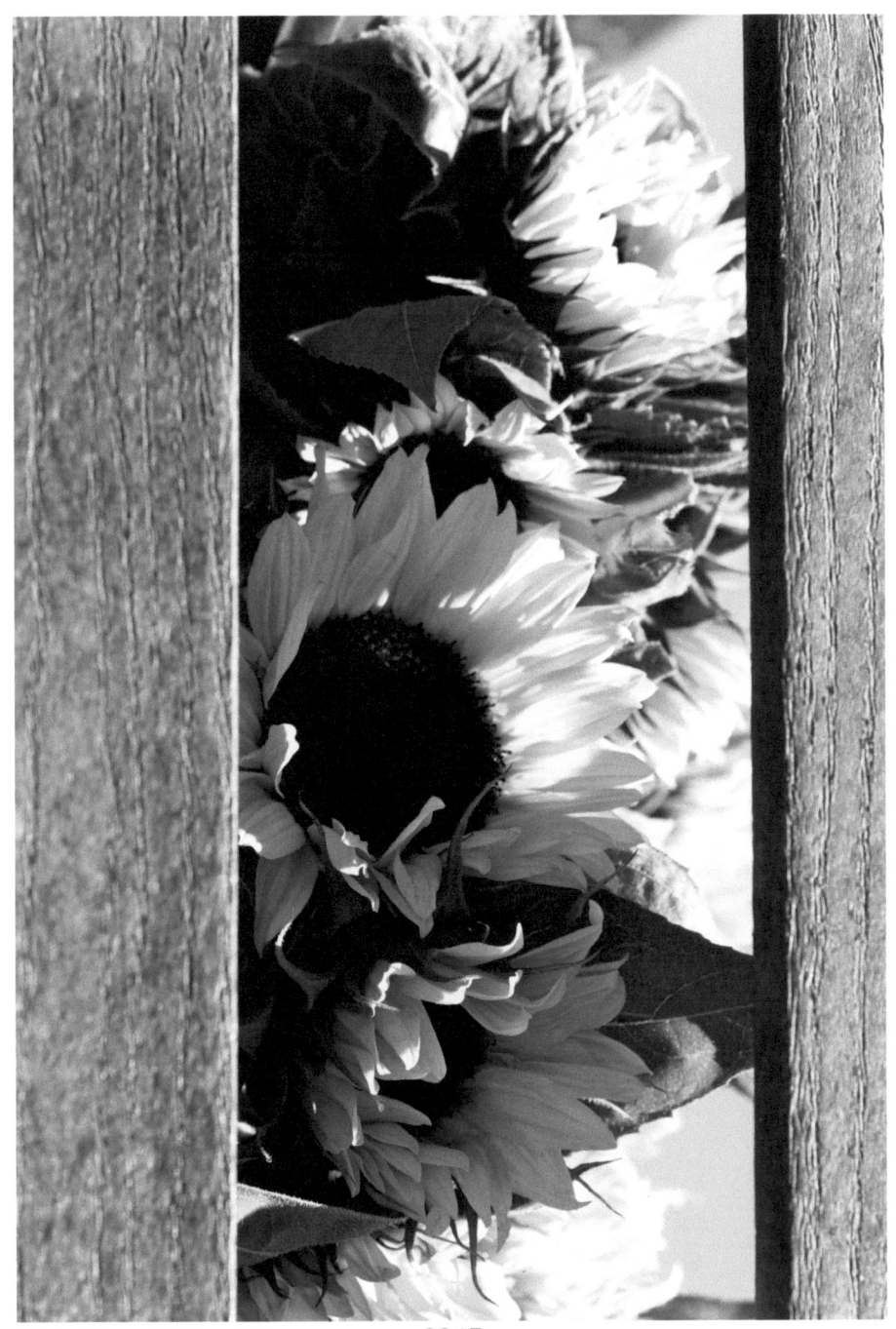

8345

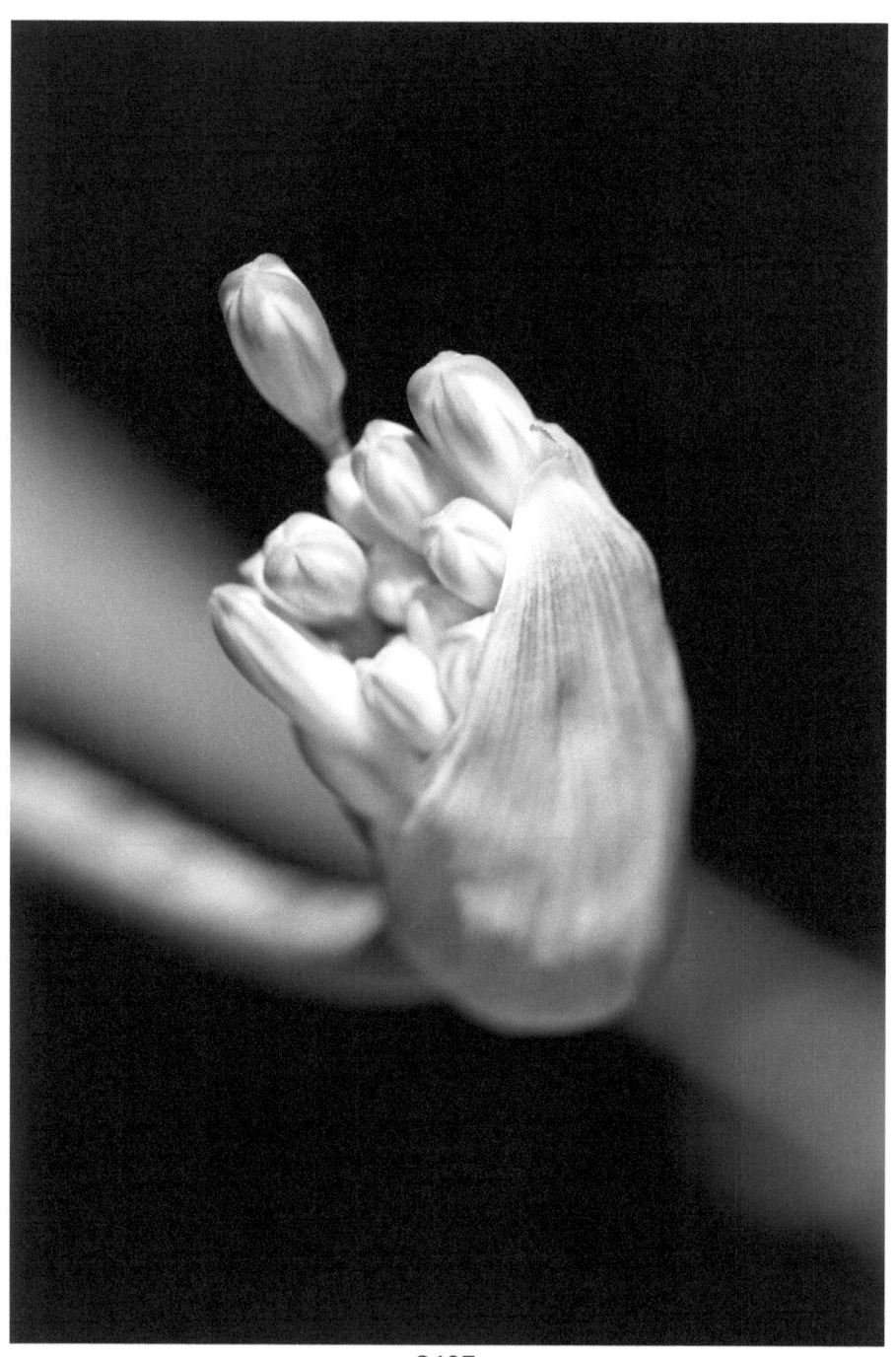

8407

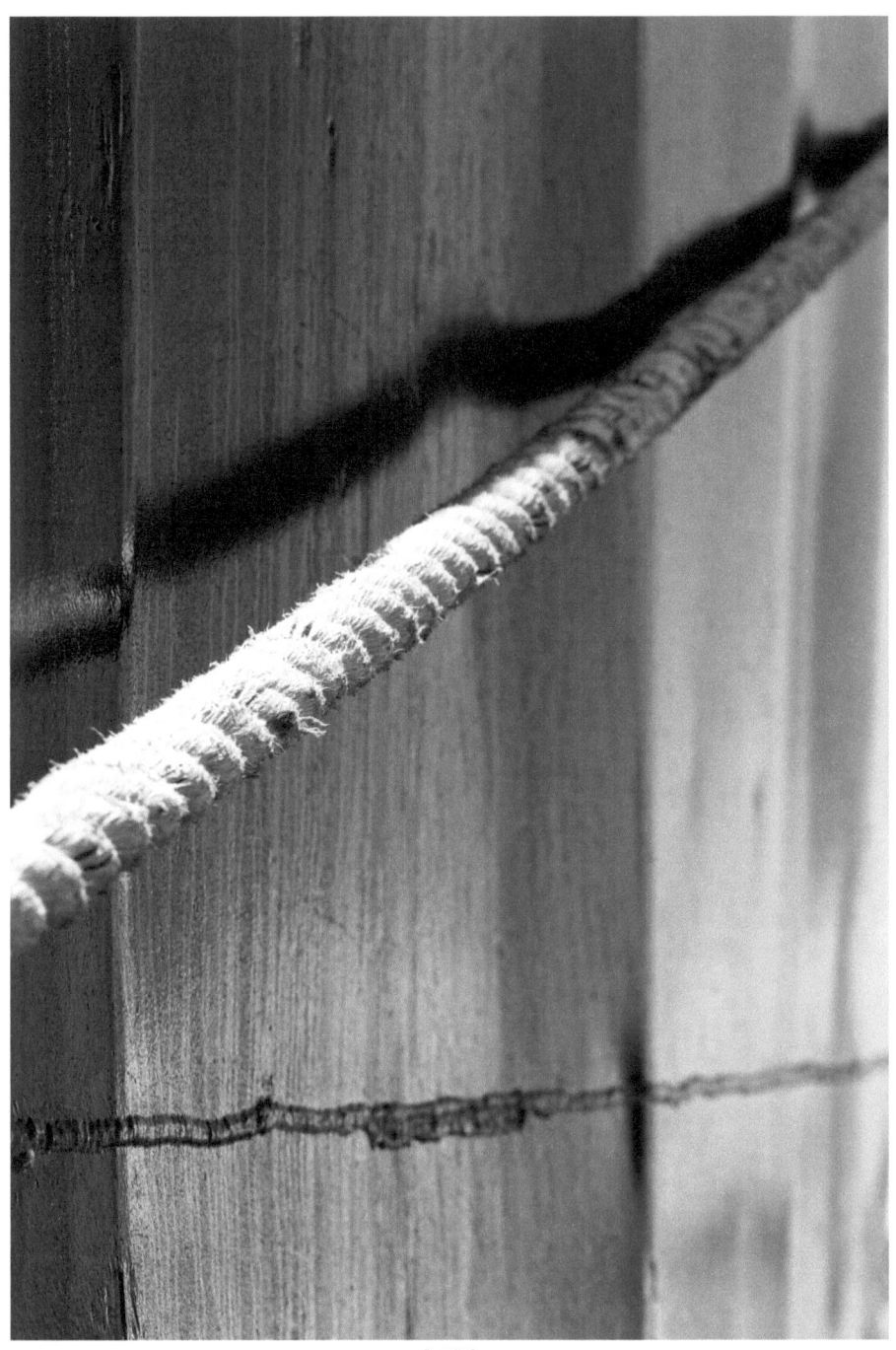

8470

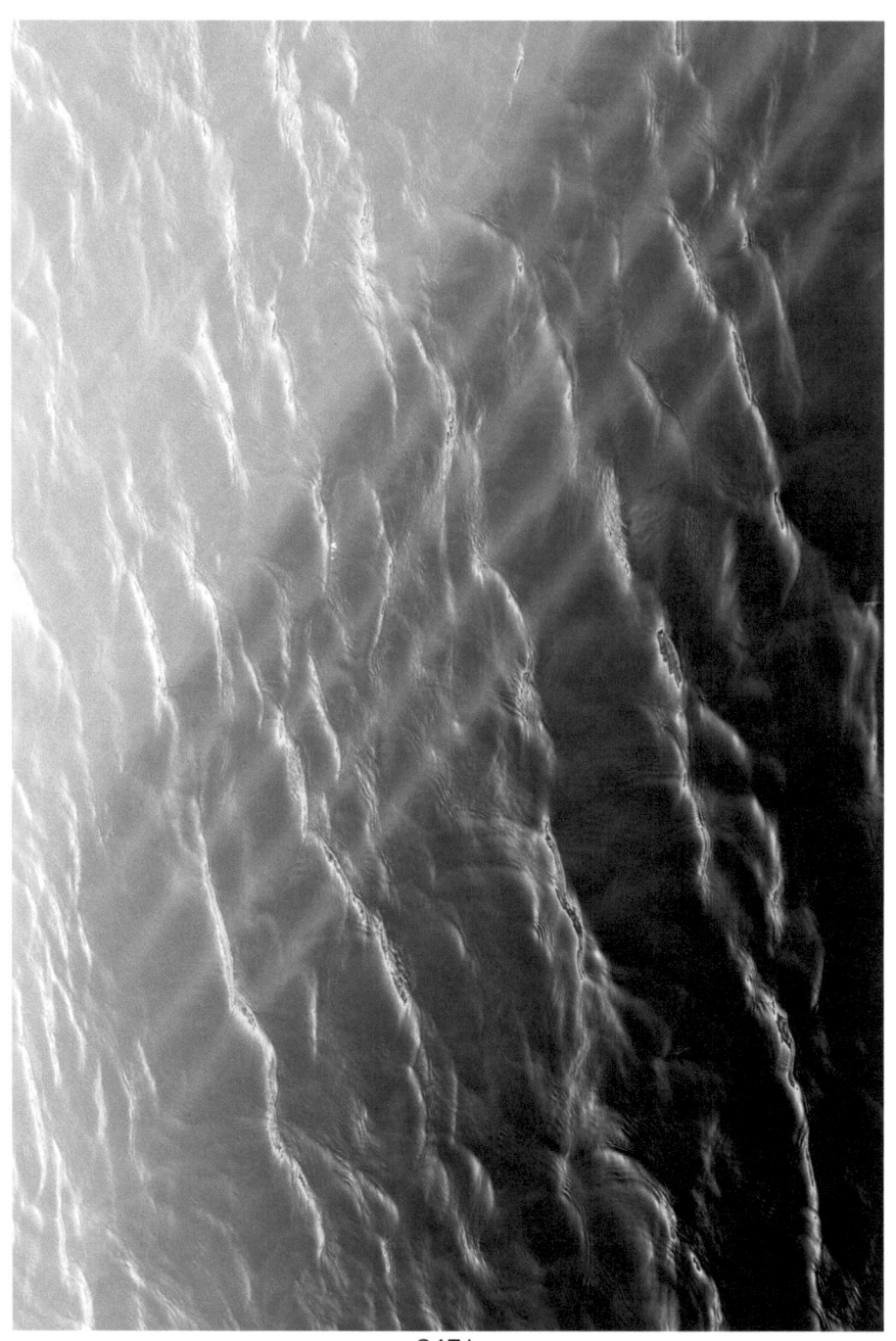

8471

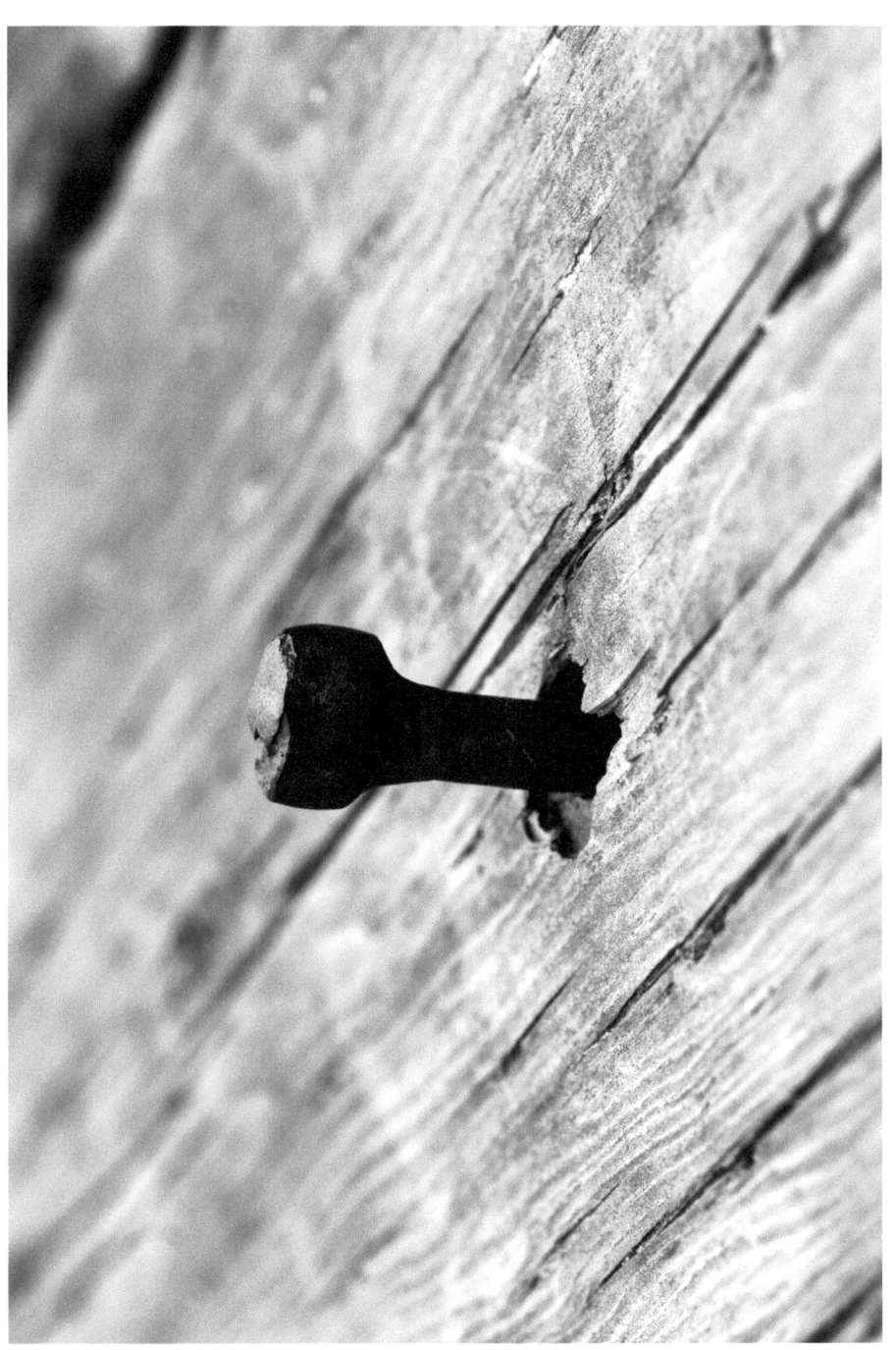

9024

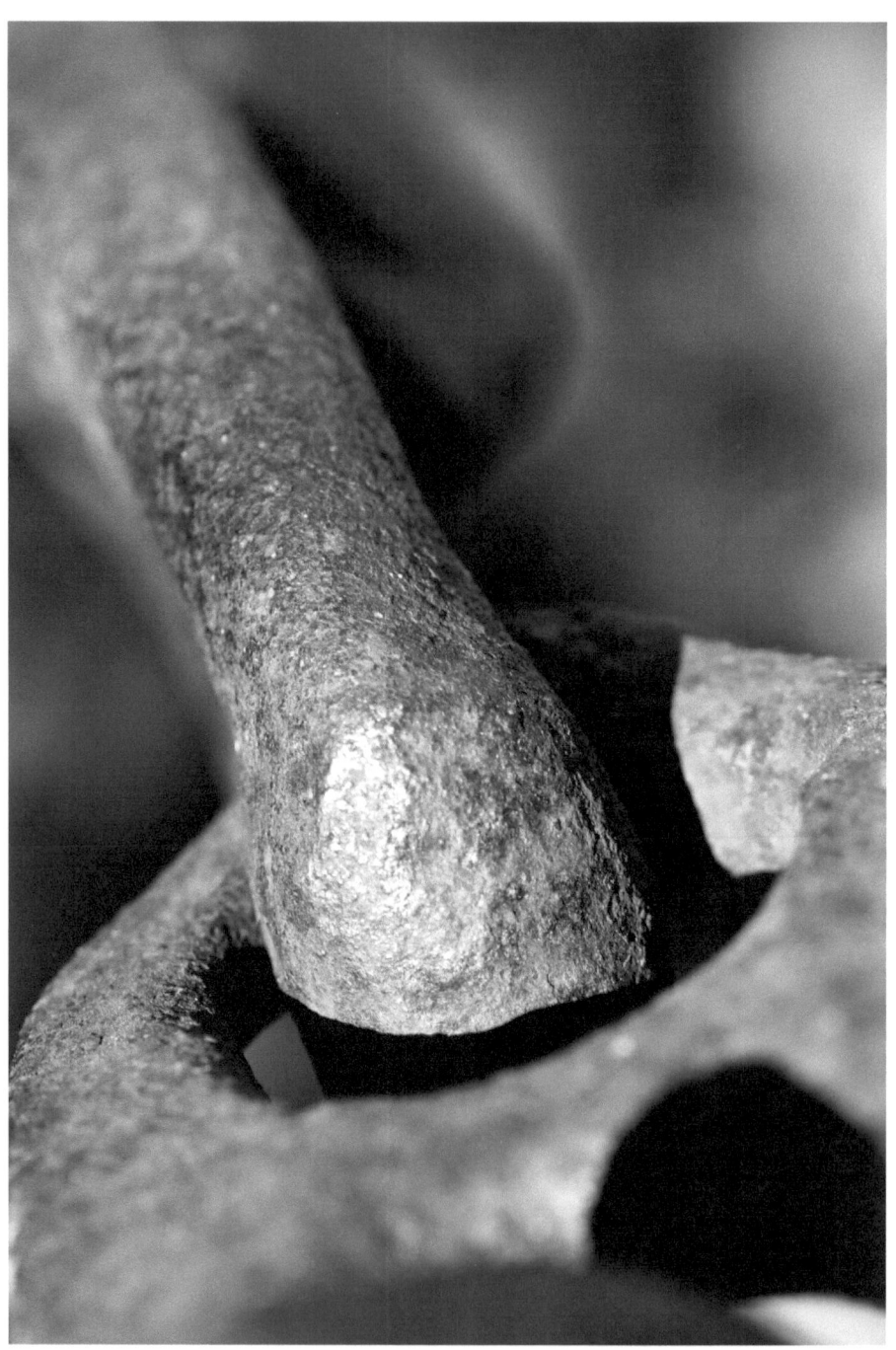

9353

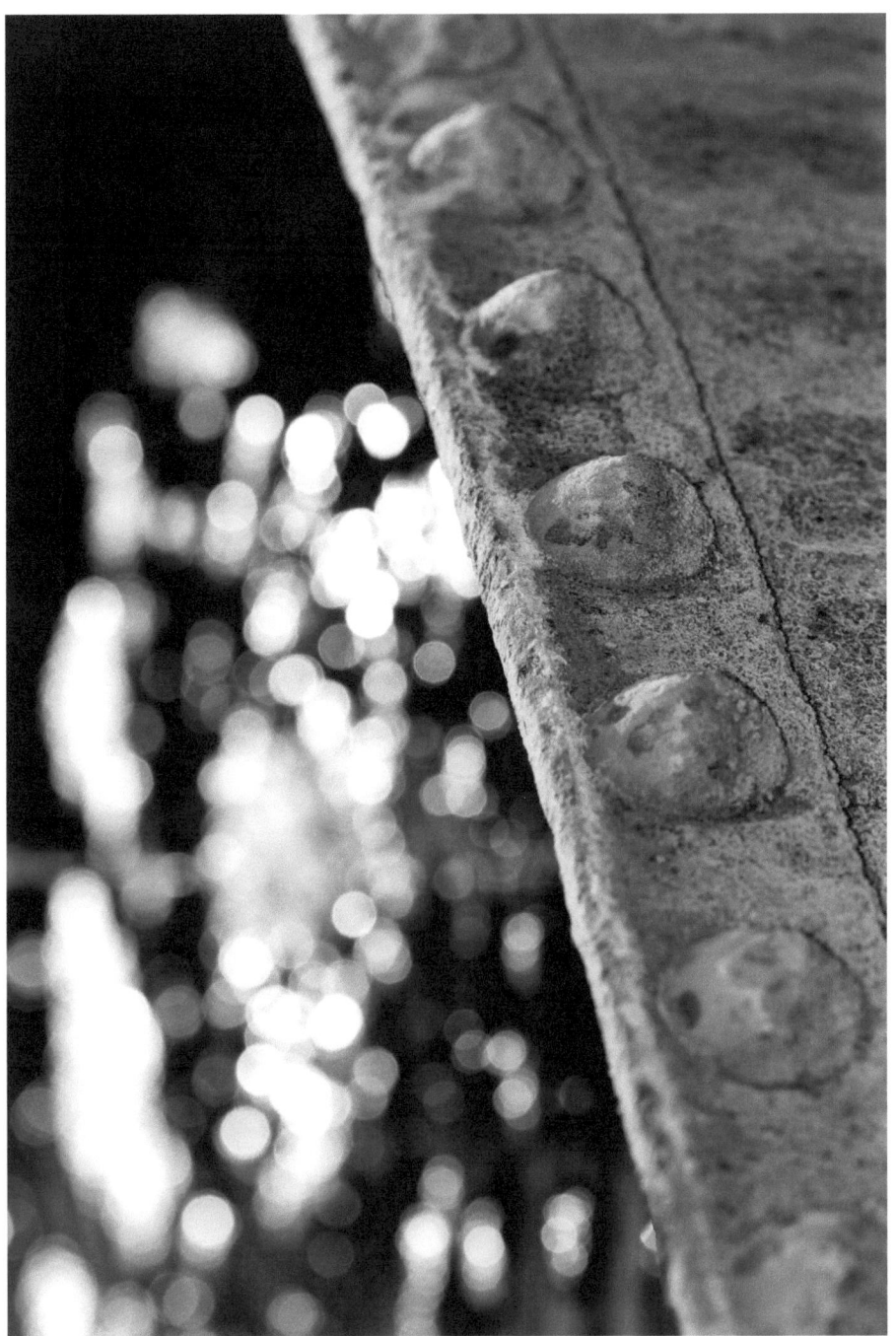

9430

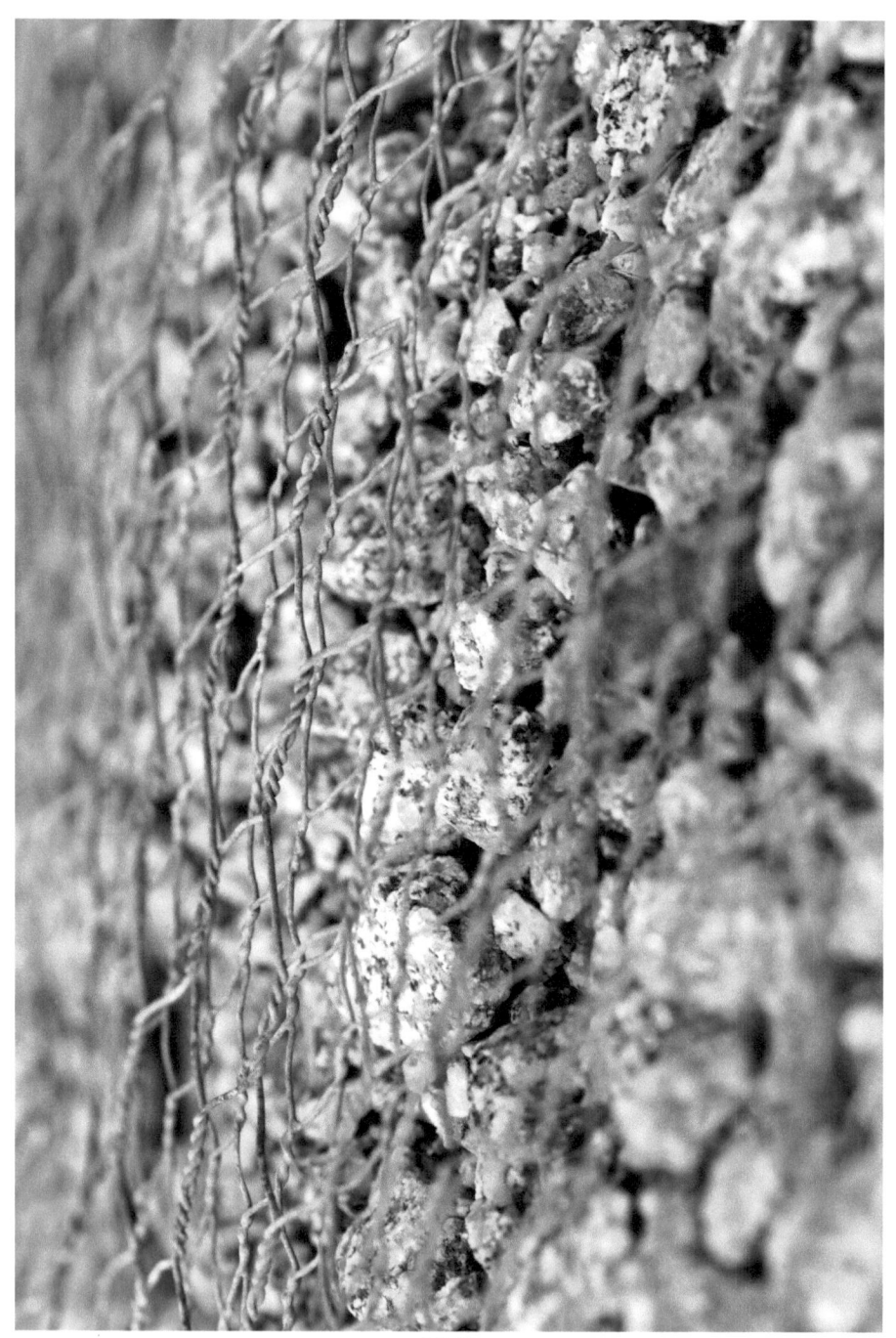

9970

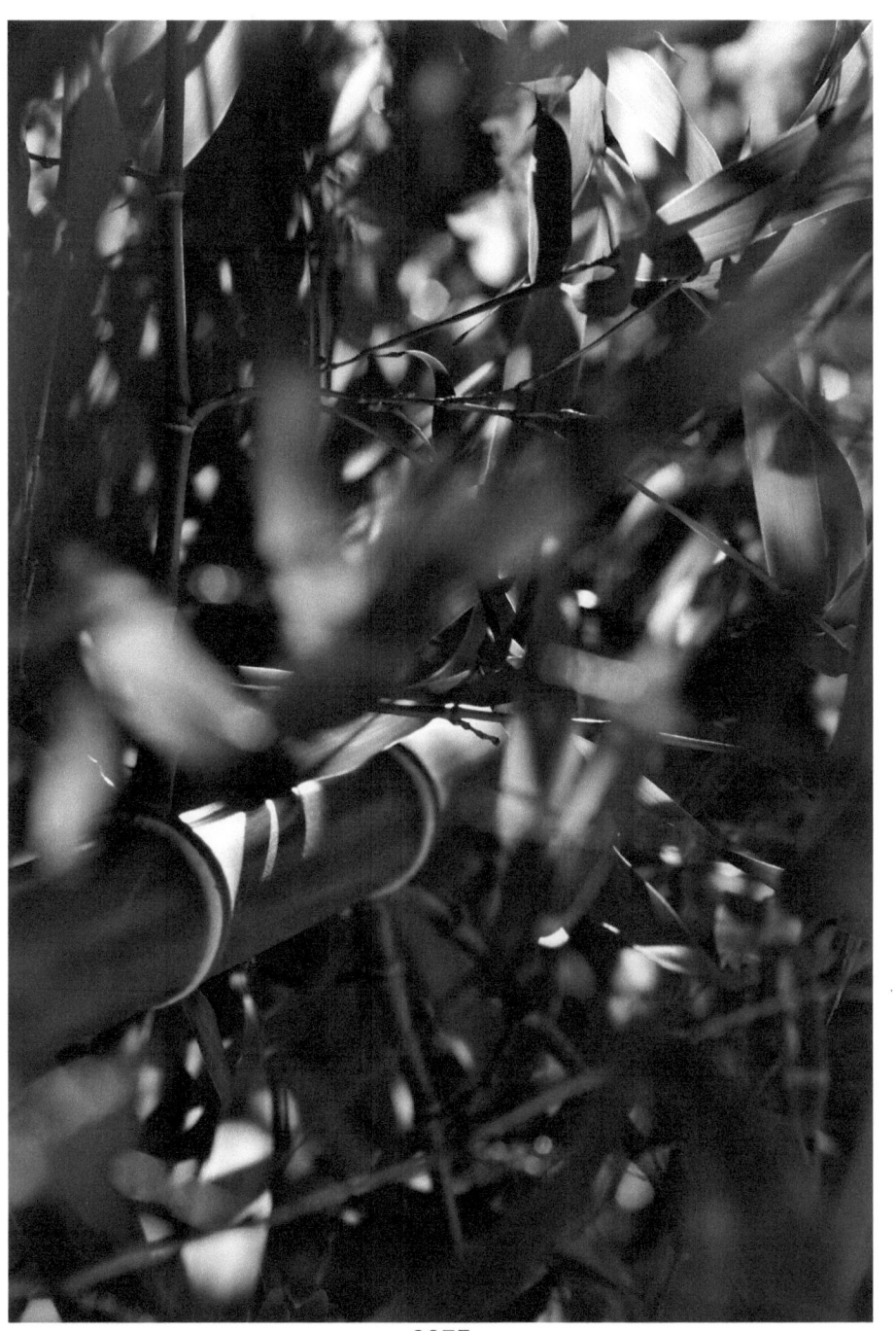

9975

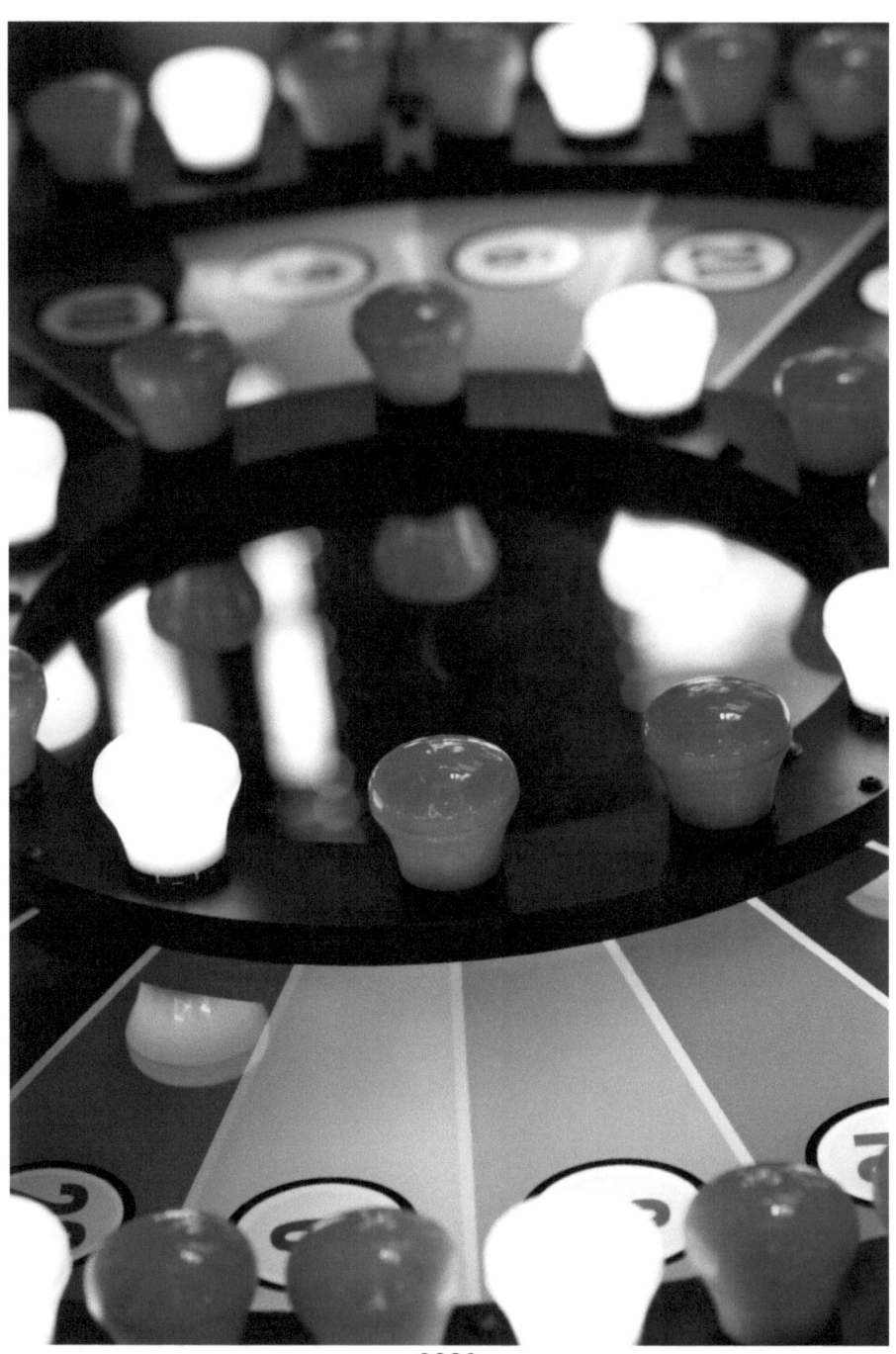

9980

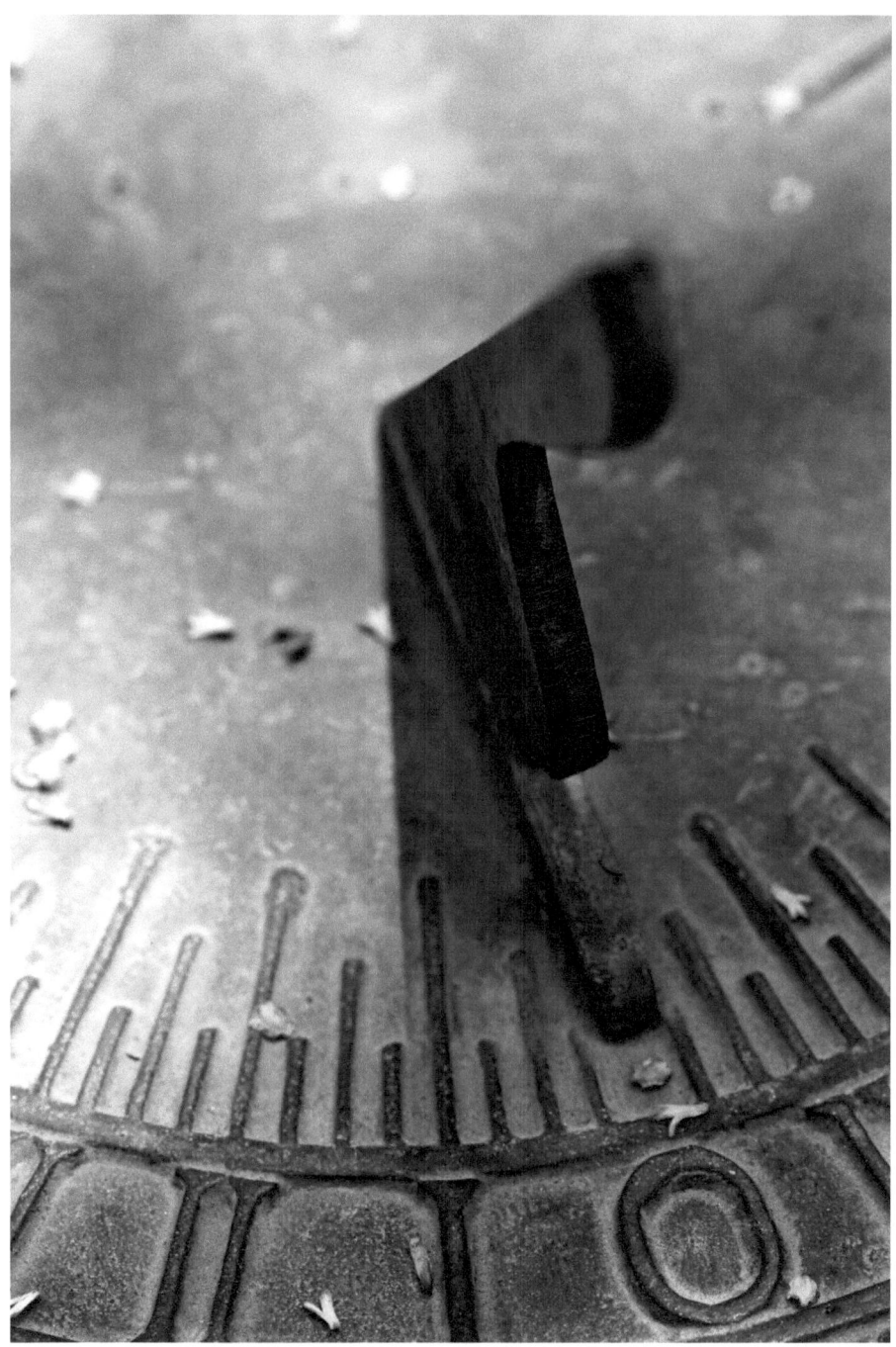

10002